THE **REAL** HEALTHCARE REFORM

How *embracing civility* can beat back burnout and revive your healthcare career

Linda H. Leekley BS, RN

Stacey Turnure, RN

In the Know, Inc. ✳ www.embracingcivility.com ✳ 919.403.8979

Publisher's Cataloging in Publication

Leekley, Linda H.

Turnure, Stacey

The Real Healthcare Reform: How Embracing Civility Can Beat Back Burnout and Revive Your Healthcare Career

—1st ed.

LCCN: 2012904267

ISBN-13: 978-0-9853222-0-5

ATTN: QUANTITY DISCOUNTS ARE AVAILABLE TO YOUR COMPANY OR EDUCATIONAL INSTITUTION

For more information, please contact the publisher at:
In the Know, Inc, 306 Brandermill Drive, Durham, North Carolina 27713

919.403.8979 ✳ info@knowingmore.com

sben   a 15951069   12/1/2016

Dedications

For my mother, who encouraged my dual pursuits of nursing and writing; and for my father, who embraced civility daily in both word and deed.

Linda H. Leekley

To my mother, for teaching me to apologize if I offend, to forgive when I'm aggrieved and to, above all, remain humble, kind and patient.

Stacey Turnure

"Always be a little kinder than necessary."
~James M. Barrie

Table of Contents

Why We Wrote this Book

Working in the healthcare environment is unlike any other professional situation you will ever encounter. The medical field is stressful, fast paced, competitive, highly technical and constantly evolving. And, because human lives are at stake, those of us in healthcare shoulder a heavy responsibility.

When all these factors combine, workers tend to feel powerless, stressed out, depressed and even angry. People who feel powerless and angry are more likely to assert misguided power by abusing others. That's one reason why many healthcare environments are plagued by hostility, gossip, bullying and unhealthy competition—leading to a widespread *culture of incivility.*

We believe that the cyclical "shortage" of healthcare workers may, in fact, be a shortage of workers willing to work under these conditions—and we want to inspire you to make some changes.

Civility is the REAL healthcare reform our industry needs!
This book will show you how to create a
culture of civility in the healthcare field.

So, if you feel burned out, beaten up, disrespected or just plain discouraged about your job in healthcare, this book is for you.

We are glad you have chosen a career in healthcare—
and we want you to STAY!

Whether you are just entering the healthcare field or you've been providing healthcare services for years, this book offers an easy to follow, step-by-step guide to changing your outlook, improving your professional relationships, and brightening your future in healthcare.

1 Why Civility Matters

To appreciate why civility is so critical in the healthcare setting, it is important to understand exactly what it entails. The Institute of Civility describes it in the following way:

> *Civility is about more than merely being polite, although being __polite__ is an excellent start. Civility fosters a deep __self-awareness__, even as it is characterized by true __respect__ for others. Civility requires the extremely hard work of __staying present__ even with those with whom we have deep-rooted and perhaps fierce disagreements. It is about constantly being open to hear, to learn, to teach and to __change__. It seeks common ground as a beginning point for __dialogue__ when differences occur, while at the same time recognizes that differences are enriching. It is patience, grace, and __strength of character__.*

Sadly, civility has been overlooked and undervalued for far too long among healthcare professionals—and now there is proof that a lack of civility adds to medical errors, poor patient satisfaction, higher employee turnover, stress, burnout, bullying and higher healthcare costs for consumers.

Civility training in healthcare settings has the potential to improve patient care, strengthen team relationships and create an atmosphere that energizes and inspires those who are in it. Healthcare professionals who embrace civility are less likely to quit or "job hop," and are less likely to burn out, bully or "eat their young!"

Since the Joint Commission issued a statement on incivility and disruptive behaviors in 2009, survey after survey has revealed that nearly *all* healthcare workers have either witnessed or been the victim of incivility. While a small percentage filed costly lawsuits, the majority did nothing to report or resolve the matter. Why? *Because that's just the way things have always been.*

Healthcare workers describe incivility as behaviors that include:

- **Using demeaning or disparaging language, gestures or behaviors.** Unfortunately, people can demean each other in many different ways, including speaking with the intent to belittle or degrade, eye rolling, giving the silent treatment and using sarcasm.

  Example: Susan asks the receptionist if she has any messages from the doctor. The receptionist rolls her eyes, sighs heavily and replies, "If you have a message, you will know because I will hand you one of these cute little blue slips. Okay?"

- **Gossip and slander.** Gossip involves spreading rumors or speaking negatively about another person. Making false statements intended to damage the reputation of another can be considered slander.

  Example: Two co-workers are talking in the break room when their supervisor walks in. Because they know they will be overheard, they intentionally mention that they think a third co-worker is having an affair with someone in management.

- **Intimidation.** People intimidate others by intentionally using *fear* to manipulate them. Intimidation may include yelling, invading personal space, throwing things, slamming things and losing one's temper.

  Example: The doctor asks Joe if his patient has had the physical therapy consultation that he ordered earlier. Joe says he doesn't know but will check the chart. The doctor throws the chart at Joe and yells, "Here, go ahead and check it. But, I can tell you it's not in there because it didn't happen. You need to explain yourself right now!"

- **Sabotaging.** Sabotage involves setting someone up to fail or intentionally creating a situation to make another person look foolish or incompetent.

  Example: Julie does not like Vic. From the day he was hired, she has made it her mission to get rid of him. One day, after the doctor writes an order for one of Vic's patients, Julie intentionally moves the chart so that Vic will miss the new order and get written up—or fired.

- **Bullying.** A bully uses power to intimidate or harm someone.

  Example: Rob and Bill are both candidates for a promotion that just opened up. They both submit their resumes and schedule interviews. When Bill is given the position, Rob waits for him outside by his car. He tells him, "I'd watch my back if I were you. I don't know what lies you told those people, but I should have gotten that job. If I ever find out you said something bad about me, you'll pay."

- **Offensive written communications.** This includes emails, letters, notes, and social media messages used to inflict physical or emotional harm.

  Example: Tonya updates her Facebook status one day. It reads, "I'm not naming any names, but a certain little blonde b**** who makes up the schedules at work is gonna get it if she puts me down for one more Saturday."

- **Hate-ism (Rankism, Racism, Ageism, Sexism).** Intentionally targeting a victim based on rank, age, gender, race or sexual orientation are all examples of profiling because of an "ism."

  Example: Sandra works in HR. She reads through, sorts and decides the fate of every resume and job application that comes into the facility. She doesn't admit this to anyone, but she purposely "loses" applications from people with Hispanic sounding last names. She tells herself they're probably illegal anyway and that they should just go back to their own country to work.

The Cost of Incivility in Healthcare

The cost of incivility is high—and money is not the only way we pay. Healthcare workers pay for incivility with their mental health. Patients pay for incivility with their physical health. Organizations pay for incivility with their profit margins. In their book, *The Cost of Bad Behavior: How Incivility Is Damaging Your Business and What to Do About It*, authors Pearson and Porath found that workers' stress resulting from incivility costs corporations throughout the U.S. as much as $300 billion a year.

The mental health toll that incivility takes on workers can be seen in decreased morale, lower self-esteem and increased diagnoses of anxiety, depression and even post-traumatic stress disorder.

Working in a culture of incivility leads to more absenteeism. Researchers found that 47% of respondents reported spending less time at work because of incivility. Absenteeism in healthcare leads to dangerous staffing ratios, and unsafe staffing ratios cause poor quality of care and an increase in medical errors.

Twelve percent of victims admit they have quit a job because of incivility. Employees who quit really run up the tab for healthcare organizations because it can cost anywhere from 1.5 to 2.5 times the worker's annual salary to recruit and train a replacement.

✳ Using this Book for Civility Training ✳

"To assure quality and to promote a culture of safety, healthcare organizations must address the problem of behaviors that threaten the performance of the healthcare team."
~ The Joint Commission

When it became clear that incivility was a patient safety issue, the Joint Commission stepped in to regulate the problem and offer some solutions. One of the Commission's key recommendations includes education for all staff on appropriate professional behavior. *This book is the answer to that recommendation. It provides the education.*

"All intimidating and disruptive behaviors are unprofessional and should not be tolerated."
~ The Joint Commission

The following chapters will lead you on a personal journey toward embracing civility and using it to resolve the (mostly unspoken) problems that may be breeding a culture of incivility in your workplace.

It Starts with You!

"There is only one corner of the universe you can be certain
of improving...and that's your own self."
~Aldous Huxley

Healthcare is a people-oriented business, so it stands to reason that getting along with co-workers is part of your job. Sometimes, it's the hardest part! You may be tempted to gripe about how this person is rude or that person is lazy—and you might even be right. But, other people's actions are beyond your control.

You are responsible *only* for yourself. Every word you speak and every action you take boils down to this: they are the individual *personal decisions* that you must make every day.

Think of your life and your job as your own personal corporate empire and you are the Chief Executive Officer. In order to successfully run the empire, the CEO must manage the company's products.

Your own civility (the way you interact with others and the way you manage your moods and emotions) is your "product." So, ask yourself, "How well am I managing my product?" For example:

- Can I feel and express anger or frustration without hurting others—and then let it go?

- Can I accept and even appreciate that other people have needs and opinions which are different from my own?

- Can I encourage and enjoy the successes of others?

- Do I actively seek out ways to feel personally empowered and avoid trying to dominate people whom I perceive to be weaker?

- Do I avoid participating in dangerous gossip and bullying behaviors?

- Am I able to recognize when someone else feels angry or frustrated and keep myself from reacting impulsively in response?

If you really want to be a part of creating a culture of civility in the healthcare workplace, then it HAS to start with you. If you answered no to any of the questions above, you have some work to do on yourself—before you can expect anything else to change.

Everything You Do Matters

The first step toward civility is to realize that everything you say and do impacts your life—and all the people in it.

"For every action, there is an equal and opposite reaction."
~ Newton's 3rd Law of Motion

When Sir Isaac Newton wrote his 3rd law of motion, he was thinking about how physical objects act and react upon each other. For example, if you throw a tennis ball at a brick wall, it will hit the wall and bounce back to you. There is an equal and opposite reaction. The ball is traveling in one direction; then it hits the wall and travels in the *opposite* direction (back to you) with the same, or equal, force that you threw it.

The great thing about Newton's law is that it can be applied to life as well. Any action, emotion or attitude that you throw out to the world will come back to you. For example, if you are mean and short-tempered, then people will probably be mean and short-tempered with you. If you are kind and patient, then people tend to be kind and patient in return.

So if you want to be treated kindly, fairly and with respect, you must embrace civility and treat others kindly, fairly and with respect.

"[Newton's 3rd Law is] the Golden Rule to the tenth power!"
~Oprah Winfrey

The question is: How can you be kind, fair and respectful all the time when life and work can be so stressful—and just plain hard?

You do it by embracing civility! Civility requires you to become more self-aware so that you control your attitude, manage your moods and choose behaviors that do not negatively impact your life or disrupt those around you.

How's Your Attitude?

"The only difference between a good day
and a bad day is your attitude."
~Dennis S. Brown

Did you know that when you are face-to-face with people, your attitude is the first thing they pick up on? Before you even say a word, the people around you get clues from you about how you are feeling.

Consider this: Two co-workers walk in the door at the same time. Jim gives you a big smile and says, "Good morning! It's great to see you today!" Carol has a frown on her face and walks by you without saying a word. Would you rather spend the day working with Jim or with Carol? And, if you were a patient, which person would you rather have caring for you?

So, what exactly is an "attitude" and what can people do to keep it positive? An attitude is a mental inclination that develops based on the beliefs, values and assumptions that we hold. One simple analogy is that if you were raised to "count your blessings" or to look at the "bright side" of life, you may be inclined to view life with an optimistic, hopeful state of mind. Or, if your past life experiences taught you to expect bad things to happen or to look at the glass as "half empty" instead of half full, you may have a more pessimistic mental attitude.

The good news is that our attitudes are habits—and habits can be changed. Each of us has a choice about whether we want to view the world with a cheerful outlook or a sour mindset.

Now, think about your co-workers. **Put yourself in their shoes for a minute and answer these questions:**

- How do you think they feel every day when you come to work?

- Are they glad to see you because they know you will be pleasant to be around?

- Do they know that you take your *work* seriously—but not yourself?

- Is your workplace better because you are there?

You probably spend more waking hours with your co-workers than with your family. If you don't bring a positive attitude to your workplace, you are wasting a big part of your life being unhappy. And keep in mind that happiness is contagious! If you come to work happy and you spread those good feelings around, they will rub off on everyone around you.

Working with patients who are sick, and sometimes dying, can be depressing. Bringing a positive attitude with you to work every day can help balance out the sadness that is part of every healthcare worker's job. Being professional means that you use your knowledge and skills to perform your job well. Embracing civility on the job means that you keep things positive—using qualities like kindness, consideration and a sense of humor to get along with both patients and co-workers.

There's No Escaping It

Just like the "shin bone's connected to the knee bone and the knee bone's connected to the thigh bone," your attitude links squarely to your emotions—and your emotions affect how you feel *physically*. Consider these facts about a simple smile:

- The muscles you use to smile send messages back to the brain telling it to feel happy.

- Women smile eight times more often than men—and women live about eight years longer than men. Coincidence?

- Smiling actually *cools down* your brain while frowning heats it up.

- It takes a lot more energy to frown than it does to smile. You use about 60 muscles for a frown but as few as 17 muscles for a smile. So, frowning zaps your energy!

Improve Your Self-Awareness

Take notice of how your emotions affect you physically. For example, do you get a headache or a stomach ache when you are stressed? Do your palms sweat or your hands shake when you are nervous? Having a physical reaction to an emotion is normal. But, being aware of the reaction can help you *control* it.

Draw a line from each of the emotions listed below to the place on your body where you "feel" it. If you don't know, take time to pay attention over the next few days and come back to this page when you figure it out!

HAPPY	ANGRY
CHEERFUL	STRESSED
EMBARRASSED	NERVOUS
FRIGHTENED	SAD
EXHAUSTED	HEARTBROKEN
CREATIVE	ANNOYED
JEALOUS	WORRIED

Keep Improving Your Self-Awareness

Your emotions influence your behavior. You just "connected the dots" between a list of 14 emotions and the physical feelings they evoke. Now, take a look at how these same emotions affect your behavior.

For each of the feelings listed below, write a brief description of how your behavior changes as a result of the emotion. For example, when you are sad, do you overeat or watch too much television? When you are mad at your spouse, do you yell at your children? When you are stressed about money, do you become grouchy or short-tempered at work?

When I am EMBARRASSED, I usually _____

When I am EXHAUSTED, I usually _____

When I am JEALOUS, I usually_____

When I am ANGRY, I usually _____

When I am STRESSED, I usually_____

When I am NERVOUS, I usually_____

When I am SAD, I usually _____

When I am HEARTBROKEN, I usually _____

When I am ANNOYED, I usually _____

When I am WORRIED, I usually_____

Manage Your Moods!

Understand how your behavior affects others. Everything you say and do has an effect on the people around you. For example, you just paid your monthly bills and realize you don't have enough money to sign your daughter up for the softball team she wants to join. You are stressed, embarrassed and angry. You arrive at work to find a group of co-workers laughing in the break room. Their happiness annoys you and you lash out.

In the last activity you looked at how your emotions affect your behavior. Now, take a look at how those behaviors affect your family, your co-workers and even your patients. Choose two or three emotions and behaviors from the previous page and fill in the blanks:

EMOTION #1

The EMOTION: _____

My BEHAVIOR: _____

The EFFECT my behavior has on others:_____

_____

EMOTION #2

The EMOTION: _____

My BEHAVIOR: _____

The EFFECT my behavior has on others:_____

_____

EMOTION #3

The EMOTION: _____

My BEHAVIOR: _____

The EFFECT my behavior has on others:_____

_____

More on Managing Your Moods

What can you do differently? Being able to manage your moods does not mean you ignore your feelings, nor should you minimize or feel ashamed of those feelings. Managing your moods just means you recognize your own emotions and choose behaviors that prevent any negative impact on you or the people around you.

Read the following alternative behaviors and place a checkmark next to any you might like to try the next time you experience a difficult emotion. Keep in mind, the idea here is to "Do No Harm." The goal is to channel the energy of negative emotions into a positive and productive outcome.

❑ Get outside; take a walk.

❑ Call your best friend, your mother or your spouse.

❑ Go for a drive and drive safely!

❑ Meditate or pray.

❑ Take some deep breaths.

❑ Count to ten—slowly.

❑ Sing or hum your favorite song.

❑ Apologize to someone you've hurt.

❑ Hug your patient / kid / pet.

❑ Play with your children.

❑ Force a smile until you mean it.

❑ Clean or organize something!

❑ Do something extra for a patient—like paint her nails.

❑ Play an instrument, if you are a musician (or want to be!).

❑ Laugh. Find humor in something.

❑ Help someone in need.

❑ Thank someone and mean it.

❑ _____

❑ _____

❑ _____

Now write down a few ideas of your own! Think about some things you can do at work and at home to manage negative emotions in a positive way.

Being Civil to Yourself

If you're like most people, up to 75 percent of your daily conversation has a negative edge. This includes self-talk, the "conversation" that goes on inside your head. To truly embrace civility, it's important to stop the trash talking and give yourself a "mental hug" instead.

Picture this: You are having lunch with your best friend who is telling you about a mistake she made at work. You say to her, "You're so dumb! You screw up constantly!" In reality, those harsh words would never come out of your mouth because you care about your friend and would want support her. Yet, do you ever talk to *yourself* that way? Chances are, you do.

Because there is no on/off switch for the brain, self-talk continues throughout every waking moment. All day long, for every four things you tell yourself, three of them are probably negative! That barrage of discouraging talk gets in the way of managing your emotions and behaviors. And, when you repeat a negative statement or thought over and over again (such as "I hate my job"), you begin to believe it.

So, how civil are you to yourself? Try this simple activity: **First, list five negative things about yourself. Then list five positive things.**

5 things I <u>dislike</u> about myself:

_____

_____

_____

_____

_____

5 things I <u>love</u> about myself:

_____

_____

_____

_____

_____

Which list took longer? Which do you *believe* more? Can you think of ways to turn your negative self-talk into a civil embrace?

Here are some easy ways to flip negative talk into something more upbeat. (And, as an added benefit, look at how the positive approach gives you more *control* over your actions and your life.)

NEGATIVE	POSITIVE
I've got a *problem*.	This situation is an *opportunity*.
I *failed* today.	Today was a *learning experience*.
I *have to* work with that grumpy nurse.	I *choose to* brighten my co-worker's day.
That's *just the way I am*.	I can *choose to change*.
She *makes me* SO mad!	I *control* my own feelings.

In addition to creating a culture of civility, being a positive thinker offers many other benefits. For example, research has shown that optimistic people live longer than pessimistic people, avoid depression, handle stress and hardship better and get sick less often. Add health *and* civility to your life by:

- Checking your thoughts frequently. Try to catch (and stop) yourself when you think negatively.

- Turning any negative thoughts around. For example, instead of thinking, "I hate my job" give yourself that mental hug by telling yourself, "I chose this profession to make a difference. When I leave work today, I'm going to list five ways that I did just that." Now, you've spun a chronic complaint into a challenge—and created a new way of looking at your work day.

- Being gentle with yourself. Don't say anything to yourself that you wouldn't say to anyone else. For example, if you think, "I'm stupid for messing up my documentation!" reverse that thought into, "What can I learn from this situation?" Or, instead of thinking, "My supervisor hates me." turn it around by thinking, "My supervisor and I don't always see eye to eye, but I am a professional and can find a way to work well with her."

- Remembering that **civility starts with you!**

Keep Working on It!

 Civility takes practice! During your work week, try applying the following skills. When the weekend comes, take a break—then run through them again the following work week. Keep on practicing until these five skills become habits.

MONDAYS: BE HONEST WITH YOURSELF. To truly embrace civility, you must be able to hold up a mirror to your life and be completely honest with yourself. It may be difficult to admit that you are guilty of behaving in an uncivil way. However, most people have been judgmental, jealous, rude or even short-tempered at one time or another.

- Be honest with yourself about what you are doing to contribute to the culture of incivility in your workplace.

TUESDAYS: ACKNOWLEDGE YOUR MISTAKES. You may believe it weakens you to admit when you've made a mistake...but that could not be farther from the truth!

- When you try to hide or cover up a mistake, the guilt will gnaw at you and, over time, weaken your spirit.

- If you make a mistake, own up to it right away. Do what you can to reverse any effects of your mistake. Apologize with sincerity. Accept any criticism you receive as a result. Learn from your mistake and never make it again!

WEDNESDAYS: RESPECT YOURSELF. When you respect yourself, you present yourself to the world with poise and a sense of peace.

- Remember to speak to yourself *and* others in a way that would get your grandmother's approval! Respect your body by eating right and getting exercise and plenty of rest. Take care of your finances. Live within your means. Save a little each week for your future. You're going to need it!

THURSDAYS: PRACTICE POLITENESS. Remember the definition of civility on page 5? The first sentence is "Civility is about more than merely being polite, although being polite is an *excellent start*." In today's fast paced, wired world, it's easy to forget to treat others with all the common courtesies we learned as children.

- Train yourself to look people in the eye when you speak to them. Say please and thank you. Get off your cell phone. It's bothering everybody! Stop texting when you are in a room with people. Chew with your mouth closed. Clean up after yourself. Apologize if you bump into someone. Hold the door. Give up your seat on the bus to someone who needs it more than you. You get the idea!

FRIDAYS: TAKE TIME TO REFLECT. At the end of the day, take some time to think about your accomplishments and your shortcomings. Be honest with yourself. If you had a bad day, reflect on the reason and resolve to make tomorrow a better day.

- Make a list of all the things that are good in your life. Reflect on what you need to do to hold onto those good things and resolve to keep moving forward toward your future goals.

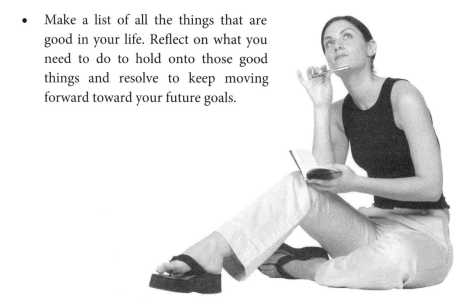

✳ **Review What You've Learned** ✳

- The first step toward civility is to realize that *everything* you say and do impacts your life and all the people in it.

- Civility requires you to become more self-aware, learn to manage your moods and treat *yourself* and others with kindness.

- Having a physical reaction to an emotion is normal. But, being aware of the reaction can help you control it.

- People who manage their moods successfully neither ignore, nor feel ashamed of, those feelings. They simply choose behaviors that neither impact their own lives negatively nor disrupt the lives of others.

- Reversing the culture of civility takes time and practice—and it HAS to start with you!

> *"If you were arrested for kindness, would there be enough evidence to convict you?"*
> ~Author Unknown

✳ **Food for Thought** ✳

- Do you believe that *one* person with a positive outlook can have an impact on a group of co-workers who have negative attitudes? Why or why not?

- Think of the personality traits that you find challenging in other people. Do *you* have any of those qualities?

- Do you think advances in technology have contributed to an increase in incivility—both within healthcare and in the world at large?

3 Do What You Say and Say What You Mean

In annual surveys, the public puts healthcare professionals on a pedestal by *consistently* rating them highest when it comes to honesty and ethics. If you are familiar with this statistic, it may have influenced your decision to pursue a career in healthcare.

So, how is it that all of us honest, ethical people became so entrenched in a culture of incivility? Is it possible that we have lost sight of our own values and beliefs? And if so, how do we get them back? We get civility back by cultivating personal and professional integrity.

What Does It Mean to Have Integrity?

Integrity can be a difficult concept to pin down. Most people think of it as honesty—or being able to tell the truth—but it's a little deeper than that.

The dictionary defines integrity as "adherence to moral and ethical principles." That strict definition paints a picture of people with integrity as "goodie two-shoes" who do everything perfectly—and that's just not true.

 Here's an easier way to understand integrity: Integrity is when your ***values*** match your ***behaviors***. It's just that simple. (Well, it's not always simple to do...but it *is* simple to understand!)

Here are a few examples:

- If you *value* promptness, the parallel *behavior* will be that you arrive at work on time (or even early) every single day.

- If you *value* honesty, your matching *behavior* will be to tell the truth in every situation.

- If you *value* being a kind and compassionate caregiver, a corresponding *behavior* would be to spend more time making sure every patient is satisfied and comfortable.

What Does It Mean to Be Ethical?

Ethics is defined as "the decisions, choices and actions we make that reflect and enact our values and morals." For thousands of years, one basic ethical standard has existed as part of most religions and has been encouraged by many famous philosophers. For example:

"What you do not want done to yourself, do not do to others."
~ Confucius

"We should behave to others as we wish others to behave to us."
~ Aristotle

"As ye would that men should do to you, do ye also to them likewise."
~ Jesus Christ

You probably know this ethical standard as the Golden Rule. The reality is that while ethics can be taught and learned by most individuals, living in an ethical manner remains a *personal choice.*

Each day you make personal choices about things that affect you, your family, your patients, your friends, your co-workers, your neighbors, people driving down the street, a man out walking his dog...wait...STOP! You wonder how your personal choices affect some stranger walking his dog?

Well, what if you make a personal choice to take your eyes off the road as you dig in your purse for your ringing cell phone? As a result, you swerve your car and hit a man who is out walking his dog. The accident changes all of your lives completely.

Many small details of life (even deciding to answer a cell phone) can involve ethics and integrity. Obviously, having integrity and making ethical decisions is vital in healthcare because human lives are at stake.

Putting Ethics and Integrity Together

What do you value? Values are all the things you believe to be of worth and importance in life. You probably learned your values at home (from your family) but you may also be influenced by friends, school, church and overall society. For example, some families place a high value on accumulating wealth. Other families place high value on charity and building a better community. Your values determine what decisions you make in the world.

How about morals? Morals are the way you decide what is right or wrong, good or bad. Your morals are shaped by your values. For example, someone who places high value on *accumulating wealth* may decide it is right to build a shopping mall (which provides jobs and makes money) instead of a play ground. Conversely, the person who values *community* may decide a play ground (which would benefit families) is the right thing to build.

In a nutshell:

- Your *values*, which are generally taught at home (and influenced by society), shape your *morals*.

- Your morals influence the *decisions* you make and the *actions* you take.

- When your *actions match your values*, you are living with integrity!

Why It Matters

Do people at work know where you stand on work-related issues? Go back to the examples at the beginning of the chapter. Say you value promptness and honesty—and you even talk about these values during a pre-hire interview. Let's say these expressed values, along with your healthcare experience, are the keys to you getting hired.

Upon being hired, you behave in a way that *matches* your values. You arrive at work and at meetings on time. You never take a longer break than what is allowed. You turn in your paperwork before the deadline and you finish all your tasks by the end of your shift.

One day you get stuck in traffic and can't make it to work on time. You apologize and are forgiven. You may get a little ribbing from co-workers who know how important promptness is to you...but overall, no harm comes from you being late.

A month later, you oversleep and come in late again. You are embarrassed by your behavior so you use traffic as your excuse—even though traffic was light. Now, you've acted in a way that *doesn't* match your values. You were late and you lied about the traffic because you needed an excuse for the behavior.

What do you think this behavior says about you? Your traffic excuse was an obvious lie to some of your co-workers who take the same route coming to work. Do you think your behavior changes the way they feel about you?

> *"He that is good for making excuses is seldom good for anything else."*
> ~ Benjamin Franklin

Tips for Behaving with Integrity

- **Clarify your values.** This is a life-long process. Your values will change over time as you learn and grow. Set aside a certain time each year (like on your birthday or New Year's Day) to write down all the things you value and how you will behave in a way that reflects those values.

- **Communicate your values to others.** You will be more likely to follow through on behaviors that match your values when you know people *expect* that behavior from you!

- **Be honest with yourself and others.** People know when you are "blowing hot air" and it's obvious when you are deluding yourself. For example, if you live from paycheck to paycheck, but wear pricey jewelry and drive an expensive car, something is out of whack. If you can't tell *yourself* the truth, you'll have a hard time convincing others that you have integrity.

- **Don't blame other people for things that go wrong.** It's your life. You are in charge. Take responsibility for your part in things that go wrong.

- **Stop making excuses.** Excuses erode your integrity until there is little left but lies. If you behave in a way that doesn't match your values, own the behavior, learn from it and don't do it again!

Clarify Your Values

On the next page you will find a list of common values. The list does not contain every possibility, so feel free to add your own!

Using the list, complete the following exercises:

1. **Decide what's important to you.** Read through the list and place a checkmark next to all the values that are important to you.

2. **Narrow it down.** Once you've checked everything that is important to you, go through and narrow your list down to your top five.

3. **Match your values to your behaviors.** Write your top five values on a separate sheet of paper. Then, write the actions you take (or want to take) to reflect each value. For example, if you chose "Nature" as one of your top five values, you might list activities such as recycling, carpooling and participating in community roadside cleanup. Following through on these actions would reflect how much you appreciate nature.

4. **Declare it!** Once you've clarified your values and listed all the behaviors that go with those values, share your list. Talk to your spouse, a relative or a trusted, personal friend about what integrity means for you. Make a verbal commitment to act in a way that matches your top five values.

Common Core Values

- ❏ Achievement
- ❏ Advancement and promotion
- ❏ Adventure
- ❏ Affection
- ❏ Challenging problems
- ❏ Change and variety
- ❏ Close relationships
- ❏ Community
- ❏ Competence
- ❏ Competition
- ❏ Cooperation
- ❏ Country
- ❏ Creativity
- ❏ Decisiveness
- ❏ Democracy
- ❏ Ecological awareness
- ❏ Economic security
- ❏ Effectiveness
- ❏ Efficiency
- ❏ Excellence
- ❏ Excitement

- ❏ Fame
- ❏ Freedom
- ❏ Friendships
- ❏ Growth
- ❏ Having a family
- ❏ Helping other people
- ❏ Helping society
- ❏ Honesty
- ❏ Independence
- ❏ Influencing others
- ❏ Inner harmony
- ❏ Intellectual status
- ❏ Job Security
- ❏ Knowledge
- ❏ Leadership
- ❏ Loyalty
- ❏ Meaningful work
- ❏ Merit
- ❏ Nature
- ❏ Personal development
- ❏ Physical challenge
- ❏ Pleasure

- ❏ Power and authority
- ❏ Privacy
- ❏ Promptness
- ❏ Public service
- ❏ Quality relationships
- ❏ Recognition
- ❏ Religion
- ❏ Reputation
- ❏ Responsibility
- ❏ Self-respect
- ❏ Serenity
- ❏ Stability
- ❏ Status
- ❏ Truth
- ❏ Wealth
- ❏ Wisdom
- ❏ _____
- ❏ _____
- ❏ _____
- ❏ _____
- ❏ _____
- ❏ _____

Apologize with Integrity

In recent years, there has been a trend toward healthcare professionals telling the truth and apologizing for medical errors that occur to patients while under the care of the medical team.

It started out as a way to reduce the number of malpractice lawsuits brought on by disgruntled patients. But, the actual act of coming clean and expressing sincere regret can have a profound effect on everyone involved.

For the healthcare professional, an apology can help diminish feelings of guilt and shame. For the patient, it can pave the road toward forgiveness and emotional healing.

An apology includes:

- Being honest about the event and your role in it, and

- A genuine expression of regret for the outcome.

Take a Poll!

 Share the information you just learned about apologizing and admitting mistakes with your co-workers. Tell them that some people think admitting wrongdoing is a sign of weakness. Others argue it is a sign of strength.

Then ask:

- What do you think? Is admitting you were wrong a sign of strength or a mark of weakness?

- What's your personal policy on apologizing?

Are you surprised by what you learned? Take some time to search your own soul for the answers to the above questions.

Stand Up with Integrity

There are many injustices in the world. Some big, some small. But, when you witness something that feels wrong—or someone or something is being harmed—stand up and speak out! You may be the only one brave enough to make a difference.

You may be showered with praise for your efforts. Or, you may never see any positive results. Either way, it's the action of standing up for what you believe to be right that helps you to live with integrity.

"Those who stand for nothing fall for anything."
~Alexander Hamilton

What will you stand up for?
For example, what will you do if...

- You overhear a doctor telling a patient that she caused her own illness?

- Your co-worker tells you she steals toiletries from the supply room?

- You learn that one of your co-workers is living in her car with her two children?

- You smell alcohol on a co-worker's breath?

- A colleague admits he cheated on his licensing exam?

- You witness your supervisor lying to a surveyor?

✳ **Review What You've Learned** ✳

- Integrity is when your values match your behaviors. It's just that simple.

- Your values, which are generally taught at home (and influenced by society), shape your morals. Your morals influence the decisions you make and the actions you take. When your actions match your values, you are living with integrity!

- Living with integrity requires you to clarify your values. This is a lifelong process because your values will change over time as you learn and grow.

- Share your values with others. This makes it more likely that you will feel obligated to match your actions to your values.

- Never make excuses or blame other people when things go wrong. Take responsibility for your role and apologize with sincerity.

- Once you clarify your values, stand up for what you believe in. If you witness something that feels wrong—or someone or something is being harmed—stand up and speak out!

"Be kind, for everyone you meet is fighting a hard battle."
~Plato

✳ **Food for Thought** ✳

- Would a huge salary raise make you happy with a job you hated? Why or why not?

- If you won the lottery, would you keep working in healthcare? If not, what would you do with your time?

- Do you have a goal for something you would like to learn? If so, what have you *done* to try to learn it?

4 Good Fences Make Great Neighbors

When you studied for your career in healthcare, you were probably prepared to spend more time with your co-workers than you do with your friends and family. But, did anyone tell you that this reality can make embracing civility a challenge?

Let's face it. Spending long hours at work can make maintaining a social life outside of work difficult. It's tempting to lean on co-workers for emotional support—especially if you're going through something difficult. The hard truth is that turning professional relationships into personal relationships can breed a familiarity that invites disrespect and incivility.

What's the Point of a Professional Relationship?

You have many types of relationships in your life. Some are personal and some are professional—but each fulfills a certain purpose.

 The purpose of a professional relationship is to work together toward the common goals of the workplace by servicing the customers, maximizing profit or productivity and maintaining or enhancing the reputation and success of the company.

This is different from personal relationships where the goal is to provide companionship, friendship or even intimacy to meet each person's need for socialization and emotional connection.

The key to building and maintaining civil relationships with your co-workers is understanding that work relationships are *professional*...not personal!

Dangers and Distractions

Melanie was the lead nursing assistant on the orthopedic unit. Melvin was the medical lab technician who came to the unit nearly every day to collect blood samples from patients for testing. Melanie and Melvin were attracted to each other and began spending work lunches together. Within weeks, they started dating. It was going well until they got into an argument.

Their relationship suffered and, eventually, they broke up. That's when things got awkward. Melvin avoided the orthopedic unit when Melanie was there. One day, he was late picking up a blood sample from a patient who was showing signs of a serious infection. Melvin's private problem caused a delay in identifying the cause of the patient's infection—which lead to a dangerous lag in the patient's treatment.

It's All about Boundaries

E.R., Grey's Anatomy, General Hospital. It's no coincidence that many television dramas center around a hospital or other healthcare environment. What is more emotionally-charged than a workplace where birth, death, sickness and surgery are everyday occurrences? Healthcare workers can develop close bonds after going through emotional experiences together—such as working on a trauma case, losing a longtime patient or witnessing a miraculous recovery. When this happens, it feels almost natural to look to your *co-workers* to meet your emotional and social needs.

In addition, the healthcare environment nurtures blurry boundaries because it remains female-dominated. For example, out of every 100 nurses, 96 of them are women. Most women want to be liked and make friends—even at work. When woman bond, they tend to share personal information easily and run the risk of giving out "too much information," or T.M.I. for short!

It's easy to blur the line between your personal needs and your professional relationships. You may learn personal or intimate information about your colleagues and you may be tempted to share personal information about yourself.

Remember, the purpose of a professional relationship is to work together—with civility—toward the common goals of the workplace. You do this by setting clear boundaries for yourself and your co-workers.

Read through this comparison of personal and professional relationships. Think about the boundaries in your own professional relationships. Are you blurring the line?

	SOCIAL RELATIONSHIP *(personal)*	WORK RELATIONSHIP *(professional)*
PURPOSE	Meets each person's need for socialization, friendship and/or intimacy.	Meets each person's need for success and achievement in the workplace.
GOALS	Socialization, companionship, the sharing of ideas, emotional connection.	Meeting workplace goals and standards.
WHAT DO YOU TALK ABOUT?	Personal information and advice are often exchanged.	Work related topics, meetings, patients, professional achievements.
RESULTS	The need for socialization is met. There is emotional satisfaction and security.	Mutual respect and trust are gained. There is a peaceful, productive and civil work environment.

What Exactly Are the Boundaries?

Here are some clear boundaries for your professional relationships:

- **Avoid spending too much time with co-workers outside of work.** For example, it's okay to have a friendly lunch when you and a co-worker have a break together, but it tends to cross the line if you go out for drinks after work or get together every Friday night.

- **Stay away from "hot topics" with your co-workers.** In general, keep your opinions on politics, religion or money to yourself. People tend to be very divided in their opinions on these topics and discussions can quickly turn into arguments. (Read more about the "Top Ten Taboo Topics" for workplace conversations on page 38.)

- **Never discuss your personal relationships or problems you are having at home.**

- **It's inappropriate to have a romantic relationship with a co-worker or a supervisor.** In fact, it may even get you fired!

- **Keep the details of your health (or illnesses) to yourself.** Of course, if you need to take time off for a surgery, your supervisor needs to know. But, no one wants to hear the gross details of your hemorrhoid removal!

- **And finally, your co-workers do not need to know the details of your social life.** For example, you may think it's great that you stayed out all night drinking and dancing in a popular new club. However, revealing this type of information may lead your co-workers to lose respect for you.

 KEY POINT: It's okay to be friendly—and you *should* be friendly—but, you don't have to be "best friends" with your co-workers.

Get your needs for friendship met <u>outside</u> of work.

A True Story

When Lauren became pregnant with her second child, she learned that her husband was cheating on her—and she was devastated.

Lauren had worked in the same nursing home for many years and, even though she was not close friends with anyone at work, she felt the need to talk and share what was going on at home. Her intention in sharing her problems was to get some much-needed support during this tough time.

But, as it turned out, one co-worker discovered that Laurens's husband was cheating with the cousin of another co-worker—and now *everyone* was discussing it behind her back. When Lauren found out this information, she was ashamed and embarrassed. She ended up quitting a job she really loved.

Think about It

- What went wrong in this situation?

- Was Lauren wrong to seek emotional support from her co-workers?

- What could Lauren have done to avoid the situation?

- Have you ever shared personal information with someone at work? If so, what was the result?

- Was Lauren right to quit her job?

- How might Lauren have handled her embarrassment differently?

- What would you have done in this situation?

Top Ten "Taboo Topics" in the Workplace

1. Politics
2. Religion
3. Sex
4. Money
5. Certain parenting topics, like spanking
6. Race/culture relations
7. War
8. Promotions or raises
9. Your plans to quit
10. Gossip

Top Ten "Safe Zone Topics" in the Workplace

1. Work-related events
2. Clients/patients/residents
3. Work-related goals
4. Your favorite TV show
5. Your kids/grandkids/pets (if positive)
6. Favorite foods/restaurants/ recipes
7. The last film you saw
8. The last book you read
9. The weather
10. Sports or other hobbies

Crossing the Line

Because of those "blurry boundaries," maintaining professional relationships with your co-workers can sometimes be difficult. You might cross the line and not even be aware you are doing so.

There are some warning signs that you've said too much or "gone too far." For example, you may have crossed the line if you:

- Share personal information about problems at home with a co-worker.

- Constantly complain about aches, pains or illnesses to your co-workers.

- Arrange special events outside of work (especially those that involve drinking), like girls' night out or going out for cocktails.

- Give personal advice to a co-worker, even if asked. Or, seek out advice from a co-worker that is not related to work tasks. Remember, unless it is work-related, giving and receiving advice is reserved for personal relationships.

- Gossip about other co-workers.

- Cover up a mistake or incident for a co-worker.

- Keep secrets with a co-worker.

- Become involved in a romantic relationship with a co-worker.

- Find yourself involved in an argument or debate with a co-worker.

"If you keep your mouth shut you will
never put your foot in it."
~ Austin O'Malley

Making It Right Again

When professional boundaries are violated, your co-workers' trust and confidence in you may be damaged. When trust is broken, it can be very difficult to get it back. And, an atmosphere of distrust eats away at civility.

Co-workers may lose trust if you:

- Gossip or complain.

- Offer too much personal information.

- Become unreliable.

How will you know your co-workers have lost trust or confidence in you?

- Some co-workers may become angry or irritated and may refuse to work with you.

- Others may withdraw or stop asking for your help.

- Your co-workers may even request that you be transferred to work in a different area.

 In most circumstances, your co-workers will not come right out and *express* a loss of trust. However, if you sense trust has been broken at work and you have an opportunity to repair it, ask yourself these questions:

- *Have I expressed negative feelings about patients or other co-workers?* Speaking poorly of a patient, your co-workers or your employer tends to make your co-workers worry that you complain about *them* when they are not there.

- *Have I revealed inappropriate personal information?* Telling your co-workers you have two children and offering funny stories about them is okay. Telling your co-worker your kids each have different fathers and neither father pays child support is T.M.I.!

- *Have I been reliable?* If you know you have been unreliable, admit this to your team, apologize and commit to becoming more dependable. You must be willing to do what you *say* you will do. Avoid making promises you can't keep.

If you answered "yes" to any of these questions, it's time to "make it right." But, how can you restore a professional relationship once the boundaries have been broken?

Here are a few tips:

- **Zip your lip.** Just stop talking about your personal life and gossiping about your co-workers. You know the old saying, "If you don't have anything nice to say, don't say anything at all"? Well, it's time to live by that motto! Limit your conversations to the "safe zone" topics found on page 38.

- **Apologize.** If you have hurt someone or caused unnecessary drama, apologize. Admit you were wrong, learn from your mistake and then let it go and move on.

Meeting Your Own Needs

All humans have the same basic needs. Renowned psychologist Abraham Maslow developed a useful way to look at basic human needs. He organized them into five levels called the Hierarchy of Needs.

Take a look at Maslow's Hierarchy pyramid on the next page. Notice that the most basic physical needs are the biggest box—at the base. Oxygen, water, food and rest are needed to sustain life. *These needs must be met before anything else matters.*

For example, a person who hasn't slept in several days is more interested in getting some rest than in boosting his self-esteem or feeling loved.

Maslow's Hierarchy Pyramid

SELF-ACTUALIZATION:
The need to
learn, create and achieve
one's own potential.

SELF-ESTEEM NEEDS:
Achievement, belief in one's
own worth and value.

NEED FOR BELONGING & LOVE:
Feeling loved, accepted and like you belong.

SAFETY AND SECURITY NEEDS:
Shelter, clothing, and protection from harm.

PHYSICAL NEEDS:
Oxygen, water, food, elimination, activity and rest.

This is how it works:

- When the physical needs are met, humans work their way up the pyramid and seek safety and security.

- Once we feel safe and secure, we seek love and belonging.

- When we feel loved and connected to others, we begin to seek ways to gain respect and recognition.

- And finally, we seek self-actualization. This is when we search for our true purpose in the world.

How Will You Meet Your Own Hierarchy of Needs?

Think about all the things you do for yourself to meet your own needs in each of Maslow's categories. On a separate sheet of paper, jot down at least five things you do to meet your own needs.

Here is a shortened example of one person's list:

Physical Needs: I eat a good breakfast each morning.

I get a good night's rest.

Safety Needs: I have a safe and sturdy home.

I dress appropriately for the weather.

Belonging & Love: I share a meal with my family after church each Sunday.

I am married to the love of my life.

Self-Esteem: I am attending college to get a better degree.

I participate in 5K races just for fun.

Self-Actualization: I volunteer at the local food bank.

I write music and play drums in a band.

HINT: If after making this list, you discover you are *not* meeting your own needs in your personal life—especially the needs for self-esteem, belonging and love—then you are at risk for crossing the boundaries at work.

Boundaries and Social Networking

Websites like Facebook, YouTube, Twitter and personal blogs raise a whole new set of questions about boundaries in professional relationships.

Ask yourself, your friends and your co-workers these questions:

- Do you think it is okay to be Facebook friends with co-workers, patients or supervisors? How might this activity affect the culture of civility at your workplace?

- Is it okay to post pictures of co-workers on Facebook? What about photos from professional events?

- Is it okay to post statements about your employer or co-workers?

- Is it okay to post statements about how tired you are at 2 am but still have 5 hours left in your shift?

- What do your postings say about your professional reputation?

- What do your postings say about your employer's reputation?

What Would You Do in this Situation?

After interviewing a potential new employee, you go on Google and type her name in the search box. Her Facebook page and several YouTube videos come up.

After further investigation you find many photos and videos of her drinking, partying and kissing random people in night clubs.

- Does this disqualify her for employment? Why or why not?

- What advice would you give this person?

Having Fun with Co-Workers

Maintaining professional relationships DOES NOT mean you can't have fun with your co-workers! Having fun at work can boost morale, decrease stress, increase creativity, lower the turnover rate—all while enhancing civility.

Brainstorm some ways you can have fun with your co-workers without crossing the line. For example:

- Share funny (but clean and appropriate) jokes or stories with your co-workers. Laughter is good medicine!

- Establish a "Fun Committee!" This is a group of volunteers who get together once a month and plan fun things for the entire team.

- Organize a monthly or quarterly potluck. Sharing meals and light conversation can be a great stress reliever.

- Plan a "Cookie Exchange" at holiday time. This is when everyone bakes cookies at home and, on a specified day, brings in enough cookies to share with everyone else on the team.

- Start a bowling league or organize a softball team.

What else can you do to have fun while maintaining your professional relationships? Share your ideas with your co-workers and supervisor and start having fun today!

Review What You've Learned

- The purpose of a professional relationship is to work together toward the common goals of the workplace by servicing the customers, maximizing profit or productivity and maintaining or enhancing the reputation and success of the company.

- When you spend more time with your co-workers than you do with your family and friends, it can be very difficult to maintain a satisfying social life outside of work. You may find yourself blurring the line between your personal needs for friendship and your professional goals. Avoid this by setting clear boundaries for yourself and your co-workers.

- Remember! It's okay to be friendly—and you should be friendly—but you don't have to be "best friends" with your co-workers. Get your needs for friendship met outside of work.

- When professional boundaries are violated, your co-workers' trust and confidence in you may be broken. This raises the risk for workplace incivility. Make it right by apologizing to anyone you've hurt...then zip your lips and move on!

"It's nice to be important, but it's more important to be nice."
~Author Unknown

✳ **Food for Thought** ✳

- Can you count on your team members to do what they say they're going to do? Now reverse it. Can your team members count on *you* to do what you say you'll do?

- Think about your workplace. How do you think that new staff members *know* if they are liked and respected? Is it easy to "fit in" as a newcomer?

- Have you ever crossed a professional boundary at work? What did you do about it?

5 Working in the Salad Bowl

There was a time when social scientists referred to the American population as a "Melting Pot." This was intended to describe a multi-cultural society where different ethnic and racial groups could come together and eventually become more like each other—and less defined by their differences.

This theory broke down when it became obvious that a society becomes stronger when people *hold onto* their differences. When a variety of people can come together and share different perspectives, philosophies and life experiences, the outcome is more creative and more productive.

The "Melting Pot" theory was tossed aside to make way for the "Salad Bowl" theory. In a salad bowl, all the ingredients come together, but each item remains unique and different. There is a quick toss—but no blending! Each ingredient retains its original form and flavor.

The population of your healthcare team is definitely a Salad Bowl! Not only are there different racial and ethnic groups, but there are different genders, generations, disciplines, educational backgrounds, personalities, social classes and income levels.

Civility is *crucial* in the Salad Bowl environment. Everyone needs to embrace the beauty and the benefits that come from all the combined differences on your team.

Incivility spoils and rots the Salad by damaging trust and breaking down communication.

A Tossed Salad of Nurses

To illustrate how easily a healthcare team can be divided by differences like age, gender, education and experience levels, consider this example of one hospital nursing team:

- **Joan is a licensed practical nurse (or LPN).** She **studied for one year** to get her license and **has worked as a nurse for 22 years.** She believes that her lengthy career makes her the best nurse of the bunch—and that more "educated" nurses seem to have lost their common sense.

- **Martha is an RN.** She went to college for four years and **graduated with a Bachelor's degree in nursing** (a BSN degree). Martha **has been in nursing for three years.** In school, Martha was taught that nurses with a BSN degree provide better care than other nurses.

- **Another RN on the team is Steve.** He **attended a community college for two years** and became a registered nurse with an Associate's degree (ADN degree). He **has five years of experience** as a nurse. Steve feels that his two year degree gave him just as good of an education as a BSN program.

- **The team also includes Betty, another RN.** She **earned a nursing diploma after three years** of study and **has been a nurse for twelve years.** Because she **worked in home health care** for years, the other nurses tease her for not being a "real" nurse. Betty feels her skills are just as good as theirs.

- **David is a new graduate nurse.** He also **earned a BSN degree** and **has just started his nursing career.** He feels overwhelmed and suspects the other nurses—and even the CNAs—don't want to help him.

And, you know what? David is right. A number of staff members see him as an "outsider" who wastes their time by asking so many questions. The only person who takes time to help David is Martha. The other nurses whisper about David and Martha, saying that, naturally, the BSN nurses stick together like glue.

In addition to these five nurses, there is **Sarah, the charge nurse.** This makes her the nursing supervisor for her shift, so her job includes:

- Making patient assignments for the staff RNs.

- Communicating with other areas of the hospital to accept patient transfers or new admissions to the unit.

- Making sure there is adequate staffing for RNs, CNAs and unit secretaries.

- Serving as a resource person for the nurses if they need help with a patient.

As charge nurse, Sarah doesn't have a patient assignment. Betty complains to the team that Sarah just sits around doing nothing. She feels that she would make a better charge nurse than Sarah.

Melissa is also part of the team. She is the head nurse—**the administrator of the unit.** She supervises and evaluates the nursing staff. She goes on daily "rounds" with the doctors and oversees all patient care. Melissa also manages the budget for the unit, trying to save money on supplies so she has enough money to hire two more CNAs. Her work requires her to be behind her desk most of the time—which causes the other team members to wonder what she's actually doing all day.

While the nurses in this example may seem a bit "over the top," you can see how conflict and incivility might arise among a nursing staff. And, because nurses work so closely with nursing assistants, therapists, physicians, social workers and other members of the healthcare team, this conflict can spill over into those relationships, too.

> *"Coming together is a beginning. Keeping together is progress. Working together is success."*
> ~Henry Ford

Being part of a healthcare team—with its various disciplines and personalities—is a unique situation that is not found in any other industry. Healthcare teams require everyone to carry an equal share of the workload with the common goal of caring for the patient.

Whether you work in a large facility with hundreds of other people or you spend your days in a private home with just one patient, you are part of a healthcare team. And, how well a team functions hinges heavily on the level of civility among its members.

What Else Can Rot the Salad Bowl?

The healthcare environment presents other unique challenges to civility and successful team work. Here are some obstacles that can hinder kindness (and efficiency) among team members:

SHIFT WORK: Most healthcare organizations function around the clock—with two or three shifts. In order to provide quality patient care, employees on *every* shift must communicate effectively with each other. As you probably know, this doesn't always happen! And, miscommunication can lead to resentment. For example:

- The day shift thinks the night shift has it "easy" because the patients are asleep.

- The night shift thinks the day shift leaves extra work for them on purpose.

- Employees from each shift are more loyal to *each other* than they are to their unit or organization.

Does any of this sound familiar?

SHORT STAFFING: With the current nursing shortage and lean economic times, many nurses and nursing assistants are busier than ever. They are doing more patient care with fewer staff members—and may feel that they don't have the time or the energy for respectful communication. For example, you might encounter a workplace atmosphere where civility has taken a back seat. The staff may be stretched so thin that they have no patience for "sensitive, thin-skinned employees who want to be treated with kid gloves."

MORE THAN ONE "BOSS": No matter where you work, you probably have more than one person delegating tasks to you. For example, home health aides may have three, four—or more—nurses supervising them in the field. Nurses may be taking orders from a dozen different physicians. Without question, it can get confusing to have more than one supervisor at a time. Each "boss" may feel that his/her patients take priority—and you may feel pulled in ten directions at once! This creates added stress and can eat away at a culture of civility.

EDUCATION VERSUS EXPERIENCE: It happens throughout healthcare. Nurses with decades of experience may feel they know more than some new physician who is still "wet behind the ears." Or someone who has been a CNA for twenty years may resent being told what to do by a nurse who just graduated school.

DIFFERENT GENERATIONS: This is similar to the conflict between education and experience. For example, a 60 year old nursing assistant may have trouble communicating with a 22 year old nurse. Or, an 18 year old CNA may find it hard to communicate with a 50 year old nurse. They just don't seem to speak the same language or have the same approach towards work!

Build a Stronger Team:
Get Creative!

Tap into your experience on the job and/or your ideas about civility in the work place. Come up with at least ONE creative solution to each of the five problems:

Communication between shifts can be improved by: _____

_____

_____

When we're short staffed, we'll communicate better if we: _____

_____

_____

If more than one person delegates to me, we will communicate better if we:

_____

_____

If I feel that an employee could benefit from my experience, I should: _____

_____

_____

If a co-worker and I can't get along because of an age difference, we should:

_____

_____

What Makes a Team Great?

There are a few ingredients that make a team great. If you're joining an already superior team, or you'd like to improve the civility of your current team, follow these simple suggestions:

- **Be kind to each other.** Working with sick or aging people can be emotionally exhausting. It can be very frustrating to work hard every day and see no improvement in your patients—or even see them getting worse. Practice civility at work! Support your coworkers...and let them support you.

- **Avoid the drama.** Keep your personal feelings about other members of the team to yourself and refuse to listen to gossip for a healthier team and a happier workplace.

- **It's not about you.** Never forget that the patient's needs are the main focus of the entire team. Be sure you (and the other team members) place the patients' needs above all others.

- **Be sensitive AND efficient.** People who choose to work in healthcare are often sensitive to the needs of others. They are expected to be warm and caring people. Yet at the same time, they are expected to work as tirelessly as a machine. It's a lot to ask of people—to be kind and sensitive and still get all the work done quickly! But, this is the goal for every healthcare worker.

- **Help and be helped.** No one can provide patient care completely alone. Ask for help when you need it. Offer help when you can. Accept help graciously when it is offered to you. One way or another, the work has to be done—you might as well share the load.

- **Listen.** Help your team members by encouraging them to talk to you when they are stressed and by being willing to share your feelings with them. No one knows better what the stresses of your job are than the other members of your team.

What Type of Team Player Are You?

It takes all types of people to make up a team. Check out the following list of personality types...you may see yourself or your co-workers. However, keep in mind these are *generalizations*. In truth, most people are a **combination** of these types and may even change types in different situations.

Here are basic types of positive team contributors:

- **The Giver:** You enjoy providing assistance whenever and wherever it is needed. For example, you teach the team new and better ways to do things and encourage the team to set high standards. Your team members see you as generous and dependable.

- **The Buddy:** You believe in the strength of the team. You know you can't do it all alone. You believe in the mission of the team but can also be flexible and open to new ideas. You are always willing to pitch in and work outside of your defined role.

- **The Communicator:** You are a good listener. You know how to diffuse conflict and keep the team working in harmony. You know how to lift the spirits of your team members and make everyone feel good about their individual contributions. Most people see you as a positive person.

- **The Challenger:** You are not afraid to question protocol, policies and procedures. You are willing to disagree with leadership and take risks when you believe something can be done more efficiently, safely or cost effectively. Most people think you are brave.

What about Negative Team Players?

Unfortunately, there may be some negative forces at work on your team too. Identifying these team members is just as important as identifying the positive forces.

Negative forces can tear a team apart, causing a decline in morale, higher employee turnover and contributing to the culture of incivility.

Here are some examples of negative team contributors:

- **The Drama Queen:** These people love to know the details of others' lives and often have no problem discussing their own intimate details. They like to gossip and tend to give personal advice—even when it is not requested.

- **The Bully:** This person likes to be in control. Bullies are strong, smart and get right to the point. When the Bully is angry about something, people know to stay out of her way or she will eat them for lunch! Unlike the bully on the playground, this person probably won't resort to physical abuse in the workplace, but may say hurtful things to injure, degrade or belittle people.

- **The Couch Potato:** These types tend to get bored quickly and are not really interested in their job. Couch Potatoes wish life had a remote control so they could just change the channel to something more exciting. When this person shows up to work, he or she does only the absolute minimum. Couch Potatoes don't really like to pay attention to details and are often told their work is sloppy.

Define Your Role and Your Goal

Now that you have some insight into teams—and you know what makes a great team— apply what you've learned to your own team contributions.

Look over the last two pages and identify your main personality type. Which one (or more) are you? Be honest with yourself. If you fall under the category of one of the negative forces, this is a great time to confront yourself and make a change. Remember...it starts with you!

_____

_____

What contributions have you made to health of your *patients*?

_____

_____

_____

What contributions have you made to health of your *team*?

_____

_____

_____

If you can't answer question # 3, list three things you can do in the future to make a positive contribution to your team.

_____

_____

_____

Feeling Overworked and Unappreciated?

 Civility among healthcare teams can be challenging. The work setting revolves around life and death, so it is rife with emotion. Healthcare doesn't end at 5 o'clock—it's a 24 hour-a-day work place. But, the bottom line is that EVERYBODY works especially hard and NOBODY gets enough recognition and appreciation.

Healthcare can be a thankless job. While you may get the occasional "Good job" or "Thank You" or even a "You made a big difference," these types of praises are few and far between.

Think back to Maslow's Hierarchy of Needs. Remember the needs for esteem, belonging and acceptance? Well, that's what you're looking for when you crave recognition and appreciation from your teammates and patients for all your hard work.

When you fulfill your needs for belonging and acceptance *outside* of work, you free yourself from the frustration of trying to get that need met at work. When this happens, you will begin to see that carrying an equal share of the workload with the common goal of caring for the patient fulfills your need for self-actualization.

You will be able to do what is necessary to get the job done—and you will feel good about it—because it is what you are *meant* to do. It's your purpose in life!

Respect: Is It Better to Give or to Receive?

"If you have some respect for people as they are, you can be more effective in helping them to become better than they are."
~ John W. Gardner

A common complaint among healthcare professionals is that there is a general lack of respect among the members of the team. If your workplace is a tense atmosphere where people neither give nor receive respect, you may feel:

- Stressed out and anxious.

- Unable to get a good night's sleep.

- Unhappy with your relationships at home.

- More injury or accident-prone at work.

- Like you get less done at work every day.

- That patients are less satisfied with their care.

- More and more frustrated with your job.

If you eavesdrop around a group of healthcare workers, you may hear things like:

> *"I'm not giving anyone respect who doesn't show me respect first."*

This attitude is pretty aggressive. Let's face it: if everyone thought that way, no one would ever make the first move! Instead, everyone would be waiting for someone else to be respectful first.

> *"I'd better show those nurses some respect so that they like me."*

There's a lack of confidence in this attitude; it's more passive. Respect is not about liking or disliking someone. Two co-workers might not enjoy each other's company, but they can still respect each other.

> *"My supervisor deserves respect and so do I."*

This is the most assertive response. Being assertive means that you expect to both give *and* receive respect. And, assertiveness nurtures civility.

Here are some tips for both giving and gaining respect in the workplace:

- **Mind your manners.** It doesn't cost a dime to be courteous and polite but it will buy you a wealth of respect.

- **Put yourself in your co-worker's shoes.** Think about what it must be like to be them—what they may be going through and why they behave as they do. When you try to understand other people, it's easier to empathize with them (even when they behave badly).

- **Pull your own weight.** Fulfill your assigned duties, but remain flexible, too! Due to the nature of healthcare, your assignment may change from week to week, from day to day or even from hour to hour. When someone asks you to help with a task that's not one of your regular duties, try to avoid saying, "That's not my job."

- **Tone it down.** If you're the loudest person in the room, you can be sure no one is listening to or respecting what you have to say.

- **Listen.** Really listen to your co-workers when they speak to you. Being a good listener is a strong display of respect.

- **You can't always be right.** If you're always right, you're doing something wrong. Try to separate your *knowledge* from your *opinions*. Allow others to have their own beliefs and opinions.

- **But you *can* always do the right thing.** If you approach your work with honesty and integrity—and do your best at all times—you will respect yourself for a job well done. And self-respect is so important. Remember the old Spanish proverb: "If you want to be respected, you must first respect yourself."

- **Bite your tongue.** Avoid insulting, criticizing, judging or nit-picking your co-workers. This behavior shuts the door on your ability to gain respect from your co-workers.

- **Hang up the phone.** Do not use your cell phone to text, tweet, surf the web or call people during work hours. Focus on the present moment and the people who are face-to-face with you in the room.

- **Be passionate about your work.** By showing others that you love your work, you become a shining example for others to follow.

- **Keep on learning.** Take every opportunity to learn new things. Observe the co-workers whom you admire the most and apply what you learn to your daily work. The more you know, the more valuable—and respected—you become to yourself, your co-workers and your workplace.

What the Heck Are You Saying?

Another challenge to civil teamwork in healthcare is communication. There can be miscommunication, lack of communication and downright inappropriate communication.

Here are a few tips for communicating with your team:

- **Learn the lingo.** Every healthcare discipline has a certain way of talking in "shorthand" about a patient. For example, a nurse might say to you, "Tell me if Mrs. Wilson asks for any of her PRN meds or if she complains of SOB." Or, a therapist might ask you, "How is Mr. Kelly doing with his ADL's? Is he moving his UE's?" If members of your healthcare team say anything you don't understand, be sure to ask what it means. They are probably so used to using certain abbreviations that they forget that everybody doesn't talk like that!

- **Don't beat around the bush.** Be straightforward in your communication with team members. The stereotype is that women say "read my mind," while men say "read my lips." Since healthcare is dominated by women, there can be a lot of communication left unspoken. Take Nancy, for example. She works as a home health aide and is concerned that she is getting too close to several of her clients. She is finding it difficult to maintain a professional distance. Nancy decides to ask her supervisor to adjust her assignment. She approaches her supervisor and says, "I've been taking care of the same clients for a really long time now." Her supervisor responds by saying, "Yes, you have. Keep up the good work!" Nancy will never get what she wants unless she speaks up for herself. Her supervisor can't read her mind.

- **Don't always say "yes" when you want to say "no."** Celia is a nurse in a skilled nursing facility. Her supervisor asks her to work overtime for the third straight day. She wants to say no, but she agrees to stay anyway. She spends the overtime feeling tense and angry at her supervisor. Her anger causes her to snap at a couple of the residents and to bark orders at several nursing assistants.

- **Think before you speak, especially if you are angry.** Charles is a therapist at a busy hospital. One day, as he is walking toward a patient's room, a nurse bumps into him accidentally. Without thinking, Charles yells at the nurse to quit being so clumsy and to watch where she is going. Obviously, shouting at co-workers is inappropriate.

- **Say thank you.** Have you ever wished that your co-workers would express their gratitude to you more often? Try sending some appreciation their way. Chances are your kindness will come back to you.

- **Learn to accept constructive criticism.** The key to handling criticism is to avoid getting defensive. Listen closely to what your co-worker is telling you and then consider whether there is truth to it. For example, could you manage your time better? Was your documentation incomplete? Take the criticism as an opportunity to improve.

- **Remember your patients.** Most people get into the healthcare field because they want to help others, right? Sometimes, this fact gets lost in a culture of incivility. In the end, sharing information about patients is the most important communication for your healthcare team. Whether you communicate in writing, with an oral report, during a meeting or one-on-one, it's all about working together for the best interests of the patient. Don't let anything get in the way of that.

Humor Nourishes the Team

When you are feeling stressed, overworked and caught up in the drudgery of your daily routine, find something to laugh about! There is no reason you can't have fun with your team! Using humor and laughter with your team can help you:

- Decrease stress and tension.

- Improve morale.

- Build and develop good working relationships.

- Build stronger teams.

- Make your job much more satisfying.

Of course there are some rules!

- Don't let humor and joking around turn into goofing off that distracts you from your work.

- Never tell "inside jokes" or funny stories about patients in front of other patients.

Humor can be an excellent coping strategy for those days when it seems like everything is going wrong. Start by finding humor in your own clumsiness or misfortune! This is called self-deprecating humor. When you can laugh at yourself, you let everyone around you know that you are human.

Know What (and When) Humor Is Appropriate

A type of humor that is unique to healthcare professionals is called "Gallows Humor." It is used to relieve the intense stress of dealing with tragedy or death—and make it feel less painful, serious or frightening.

It's okay to make jokes between co-workers during or just after a highly stressful tragedy or death. But remember...what is funny to you may not be appreciated by other non-medical people. Never let your patients or their families hear you participating in this type of humor. It could be interpreted as cruel and heartless.

When Humor Hurts

The type of humor described in the previous section is intended to lift the mood and spirit of your team and yourself. Not all humor does this.

Sarcasm, put downs, ethnic jokes and "anti" jokes (such as anti-men, women, religious groups, ethnicity, etc.) are all considered hurtful or harmful forms of humor. In addition, these types of jokes can be considered discrimination and harassment. There is never a time when this type of humor is helpful.

A word about teasing: Gentle teasing is okay if a person has demonstrated some self-deprecating humor. For example, Sandra drops a full bedpan on the floor and then slips in the contents. Afterwards, she laughs and makes fun of her own clumsiness. In this case, it would be okay to join in the laughter and tease her a little...as long as the teasing is light-hearted and not intended to be mean.

 It is *never* okay to tease people about things they are unable to change, like their heritage, age, physical features, intelligence or speech.

Build a Stronger Team:
Take the "Find 15" Challenge

In this chapter you learned that it's good to embrace the differences in all the people on your team. But, it's also nice to know you have a few things in common! Pick a co-worker from your team (preferably one you don't know very well) and try to find 15 things you have in common. Examples may include that you were both born in the same country or that you both like fancy cheeses.

The 15 things we have in common are:

1. _____

2. _____

3. _____

4. _____

5. _____

6. _____

7. _____

8. _____

9. _____

10. _____

11. _____

12. _____

13. _____

14. _____

15. _____

Build a Stronger Team:
Speak Up!

"The best way to have a good idea is to have a lot of ideas."
~ Dr. Linus Pauling

Be a problem solver. Instead of just complaining about the problems you have at work, offer some solutions! Your team will benefit from your creative ideas and your ability to solve problems.

Don't be shy about offering your opinion about how to make things better for your team or your patients. You may be able to suggest solutions no one else has thought of.

Take some time to consider the problems you face, then brainstorm two or three creative solutions to those problems. Present your ideas to your team leader, supervisor or human resources person. You never know . . . your small idea may have a huge impact!

Here's an example:

The Problem: We don't have a comfortable place to take our breaks. The cafeteria is too far away to get there and back in the short time we have. Everyone is getting grouchy because of this problem!

Possible Solutions: 1)Convert an unused conference room into a break room. 2)Take fewer (but longer) breaks.

Now, you try it!

The Problem: _____

_____

Possible Solutions: _____

_____

✳ **Review What You've Learned** ✳

- The population on your healthcare team is definitely a Salad Bowl! Incivility spoils and rots the Salad by damaging trust and ruining communication.

- Civility requires you to embrace the beauty and the benefit of all the differences on your team.

- Great teams are made great because the members of the team are sensitive and kind to each other. They avoid the drama of gossip and backstabbing and always keep the needs of the patients above all else.

- Using humor with your team can decrease stress and tension, improve morale, build stronger teams and make your job much more satisfying.

"The most important trip you may take in your
life is meeting people halfway.
~Henry Boye

✳ **Food for Thought** ✳

- If you could switch jobs with any member of your healthcare team, which one would it be and why? Think carefully. Would you pick the person who probably makes the most money or the one with the "easiest" job? Maybe you'd choose someone whose job you think is interesting or challenging? Or, would you want the life-and-death responsibilities of a physician? The decision may not be so simple!

- In a recent National Nursing Assistant Survey, only half of the CNAs said that they received positive feedback from the nurses at work. How does that compare to your workplace? What do you think can be done to improve this statistic?

6 Eliminate Gossip and Bullying

Sure, workplace gossip and bullying happen in just about every work situation imaginable. In fact, a recent survey found that a whopping 37 percent of the U.S. workforce has been bullied at work at some point. This means that 54 million employees have experienced workplace aggression! But, are there *really* bullies working in healthcare? You bet.

Working in the healthcare field can be rewarding—but stressful. Patients are sicker than ever; the hours are long and hard; the rate of employee turnover is high; and there are increased expectations for specialty certifications or advanced degrees. In addition, information changes at the speed of light which places pressure on workers to stay up-to-date on new technologies, procedures and medications.

High stakes and constant change can leave workers feeling overwhelmed and powerless. When this happens, bullying may develop as a coping strategy.

Unfortunately, workplace gossip and bullying in healthcare has a long history of ***denial***. No one wants to believe that the same people the public votes as the most "honest and ethical" professionals could or would behave with such incivility and disrespect toward each other.

However, with all the recent media attention on bullying in schools, the world is turning a spotlight on what happens to bullies when they grow up. It turns out bullying is not just happening on the playground anymore. And, special attention is being paid to bullying in the healthcare environment because the consequences include employee stress and higher turnover rates—and can even lead to harmful or deadly consequences for patients.

The problem of incivility in the healthcare workplace is so serious that the Joint Commission recently issued new regulations on reporting, disciplining and preventing such situations in healthcare environments.

A Closer Look at Gossip

What is gossip?

The dictionary defines gossip as "casual or unconstrained conversation or reports about other people, typically involving details that are not confirmed as being true."

Why do people do it?

People gossip for many reasons. In fact, social scientists believe that groups with a shared identity, such as a healthcare team, actually *need* to gossip to make sense of the social layers within the society. Most people gossip as a means to convey information, relieve stress and form bonds.

Seems harmless, right?

And, it is...usually. Except when it's not! When gossip is used as a way to discredit, humiliate, belittle or even intimidate another person, it contributes to the culture of incivility.

The bottom line is that not all gossip is bad—
and it may, in fact be beneficial to teams by drawing them closer.
But content counts!

Having a friendly giggle over coffee with a colleague about the fact that another co-worker wore two different socks to work is harmless. Saying that same person has on two different socks because she is incompetent and color-blind is malicious—and it waters the seeds of incivility.

Consider this example:

> Joan was helping Mr. Waters, who suffers from dementia, with his personal care. He became confused and upset and threw a shoe at her. Joan responded calmly and finished her work. She told one co-worker what happened and thought that was the end of it.
>
> Unfortunately, people started gossiping—and getting the story wrong. *"Did you hear about Joan? She got angry with Mr. Waters and threw a shoe at him! Isn't that awful? She should be fired!"* By the end of the day, this story had gotten back to Joan's supervisor who called her in for a counseling session. Joan had to defend herself and started crying. Such drama… and all because of gossip!

Remember…gossip is like a computer virus. It sneaks around, disrupting the way a workplace functions—just like a virus disrupts the way a computer functions. It takes only one person starting some gossip for the entire team to become "infected." Gossip can eat away at communication between co-workers, damage careers, cause hurt feelings and create plenty of conflict! It can also weigh down employee morale and lead to reduced productivity. In fact, studies have shown that the average employee spends at least 65 hours every year gossiping about co-workers.

So what's the best way to get a handle on gossip in the workplace? Let's look at another example:

> Steve and Ginger have worked together for five years. Lately, Steve has seemed stressed out and unhappy. One day, he tells Ginger that he is having some financial troubles and he and his wife are having a hard time living on less money.
>
> Ginger runs to every co-worker, eagerly sharing Steve's bad news. She adds her own twist on the story by saying, *"No wonder he's been so grumpy lately. I think he's drinking too much and his marriage is in trouble, too!"*

While Ginger's co-workers can't control whether or not she gossips, they can let her know they don't want to participate in it.

Here are some examples of how to put the brakes on workplace gossip:

> After hearing Ginger's news, Theresa decides to say something nice about Steve. She says, *"What I like most about Steve is that he's a real team player. What do you like most about him?"* Theresa hopes that this may serve as a wake-up call for Ginger—and encourage her to speak about Steve in a positive manner.

> When Ginger shares her gossip with Mark, he says, *"It sounds like Steve needs friends to talk to. Why don't you and I go discuss this with him right now?"* This approach may stop Ginger in her tracks since she won't want Steve to hear how she has exaggerated his story.

> When Ginger tells Sheila about Steve's situation, Sheila asks Ginger, *"Can I quote you on this?"* Most people who share gossip do not want to have the story associated with them. Ginger is no exception. She asks Sheila not to mention the news to anyone.

Kick the Habit

If you find yourself spreading gossip among your co-workers, follow one or more of these tips:

- Ask a co-worker to give you a little pinch every time you start gossiping.

- Pretend that everything you say about someone else is being *recorded* for that person to hear.

- Consider how you would feel if someone were talking about you behind your back.

- Think about all you could get done in those extra 65 hours if you didn't spend them gossiping!

Your co-workers may continue to gossip; that is out of your control. However, you *can* make a personal decision to "just say no" to workplace rumors, hearsay and innuendo. It all starts with you...

A Closer Look at Bullying

What is workplace bullying?

Workplace bullying is a form of workplace violence. It is defined as "the repeated, unreasonable actions of individuals (or groups) directed toward an employee (or a group of employees), intended to intimidate, and by doing so, creates a risk to the health and safety of the employee(s)."

Bullying behavior intimidates, degrades, offends and/or humiliates another person. Usually, this behavior is carried out in front of others with the intent to make the victim (or target) feel defenseless. Bullying is a far more sinister problem than gossiping...with much greater consequences.

In the workplace, a bully might:

- Criticize your work over and over.
- Spread gossip or lies about you.

- Yell at you and/or behave in a hostile manner.
- Ignore you or exclude you from the group.

- Accuse you of mistakes you didn't make.
- Insult your work habits or your private life.

Why do people do it?

 A bully usually acts out as a means to gain or retain power. Bullying usually comes from a person in a position of power (real or imagined) and involves an abuse or misuse of this power.

The Silence of the Bullied

Unfortunately, many victims of bullying never report the problem for fear of being seen as "weak" or as a "complainer". For example:

From her first day on the job, Sarah got the feeling that Melissa didn't like her.

Melissa never talked to her—in fact, she would turn her back whenever Sarah walked by.

She also:

- Gave Sarah dirty looks.

- Bumped into Sarah repeatedly with a wheelchair.

- Spilled coffee on Sarah's clipboard.

Sarah felt harassed, but what could she do? She had no real evidence that Melissa was targeting her. While she believed that the spilt coffee and the wheelchair bumps were on purpose, she couldn't prove it.

So, what could Sarah tell her supervisor? That Melissa wasn't friendly? Her supervisor would probably tell her to simply get on with her work. After a few months, Sarah couldn't take it anymore and she quit her job.

When Sarah left her job, she left her bully behind her. But she also left the bully in a position to continue the behavior with *other* targets.

When bullying goes unreported, it goes unaddressed.

Who Are the Bullies?

Do you think it's obvious who the bullies are in your workplace? Could it be you? It would be great to just say, "Okay Bullies, listen up...you know who you are." Unfortunately, bullies almost never see themselves as bullies.

Most bullies see themselves as smarter, better and faster than everyone else. They may have an inflated sense of their own worth and importance in the workplace. They think their "way" of doing things is the best or only way. They believe that causing a co-worker to look bad makes themselves look good.

Here are some personality types that are most likely to be the bullies in your workplace:

- **The Super Hero:** This person has more experience and more education, but also has an elitist or superior attitude.

- **The Grudge Budget:** This employee develops and holds grudges and pits co-workers against each other.

- **The Rumor Mill:** This person spreads negative (often untrue) information about other co-workers.

- **The Backstabber:** The backstabber forms friendships, then betrays them with co-workers.

- **The Queen "B":** This person is a natural leader but uses exclusion for aggression. She shows favoritism to some and ignores others.

The Consequences of Bullying

"Everybody, sooner or later, sits down to a banquet of consequences."
~ Robert Louis Stevenson

Bullying punishes in three ways. It hurts the victim (or target), the team and the patients. Here's how:

- **The Victim:** The effect of bullying on the individual being bullied is not always obvious. Remember, bullying behaviors often go unreported, leaving the victim to suffer alone. This can lead to increased anxiety, feelings of isolation and helplessness. There may be a surge in physical illness (real or imagined) and an increased use of sick time.

  Bullying can also lead to depression or insomnia and some victims even report episodes of post-traumatic stress disorder.

- **The Workplace:** The effects of bullying on the workplace are many, including decreased morale, damaged reputation, loss of productivity, increased absences and increased employee turnover. These are all costly consequences for an employer.

- **The Patient:** The most devastating effects of bullying among healthcare workers are those that impact patient care. Bullying is proven to place patient safety at risk because it interferes with teamwork and erodes communication.

  Bullying is associated with increased medical errors, decreased patient satisfaction, adverse outcomes and higher costs. Often, patients are the innocent victims of bullying behaviors in the healthcare environment.

You Are Not Alone!

"All intimidating and disruptive behaviors are unprofessional and should not be tolerated." ~ The Joint Commission.

When it became evident that bullying was a patient safety issue, the Joint Commission stepped in to regulate the problem and offer some solutions.

The Joint Commission's key recommendations include all of the following:

- **Education** for all staff on appropriate professional behavior.
- Holding each staff member **accountable** for demonstrating appropriate workplace behavior.
- Developing and enforcing policies that address:
  - **"Zero-tolerance"** for intimidating or disruptive behaviors.
  - Reducing fear of retribution and **protecting** those employees who report disruptive behavior.
  - A **clear pathway** to suitable disciplinary actions, such as suspension, termination, loss of clinical privileges, and reports to professional licensure bodies.

So, What Should You Do?

If you are dealing with a workplace bully:

- **Write it down.** Keep a record of every bullying incident. Make note of the date and time and include the exact words the bully used. (But stick to the facts—just like you do when you document your patient care.) This type of specific documentation can be a powerful tool if you feel the need to report the bully.

- **Don't let the bully intimidate you or make you feel bad about yourself.** Most bullies behave the way they do because they don't feel good about themselves—and want to drag you down to their level.

- **Do your best at your job every day.** Workplace bullies *want* you to fail because it confirms their power over you. Don't let them control you. Instead, let them see you enjoying your job!

- **Confront the bully in a professional and respectful manner—but only if your physical safety isn't threatened.** Say something like, "Your behavior is unacceptable." Stay calm and don't yell or cry. Bullies usually enjoy an emotional confrontation and will keep coming back for more!

- **Look for your workplace policy on bullying.** Follow the steps outlined in the policy to resolve the issue.

- **Ask for help.** If you've done all you can on your own, take the issue to your supervisor or (if the bully is your supervisor) to your company's human resources manager.

 Bring your documentation with you and talk about how the problem has affected your daily work. Let them know that you are committed to your job and that your goal is to be a team player and provide the best possible patient care.

What Else Can You Do?
Get to the Heart of the Matter!

Everyone has experienced some level of pain and difficulty in life...even the bully. In fact, bullying behavior often comes from a place of pain or fear.

Attempt to understand your bully as a frightened and fearful person who lashes out in a misguided attempt to protect herself. Maybe she is being abused at home or feels stuck in her job because she has kids in college. Maybe she is in danger of losing her home or being forced into bankruptcy.

> *Whatever the reason (and there is a reason) for the behavior,*
> *you have the potential to turn it around in a peaceful, quiet*
> *and helpful way... just by reaching out.*

Take the first step and talk to the bully in a non-threatening way. Ask her how she is doing and how she is feeling. If she seems stressed out about something, offer to help in any way you can.

Be genuine and sincere. A person who has been a bully for a long time may have few, if any, close friends and might distrust you or suspect you have other motives for being kind to her.

Begin to build a professional relationship with the bully that is based on trust and respect. Always model appropriate behavior. When you do these things, you will watch the bullying behavior slowly disappear!

Find Your Peaceful Helpful Self

It can be difficult to feel peaceful and helpful toward a bully, especially if you are feeling victimized and helpless. But sad, victimized and helpless is exactly how the bully *wants* you to feel.

In fact, if you lash out, get emotional, storm off or even cry, you may be adding fuel to the bully's fire.

Here are some tips for staying grounded, protecting yourself and diffusing the situation:

- **Get Centered!** Stand tall. Pull your belly in toward your spine and straighten your shoulders. Breathe deeply and fill your lungs, then let the air out slowly. Find something peaceful to think about.

- **Put up your umbrella.** If someone is storming or "raining down insults" upon you, imagine that you are in rainstorm—but that you are dry and protected under your sturdy umbrella. Speak calmly and rationally, saying things like, "I understand that this is upsetting to you."

- **Contradict yourself.** The trick here is to acknowledge that you can feel one way but act a different way. For example, you may *feel* intimidated or helpless, but you can *act* strong and confident until you are able to get out of the situation. This is not to say your feelings of fear or helplessness are wrong. They are not. You really do feel that way. But, remember, that's how the bully wants you to feel. Don't fulfill the bully's wishes!

Write Your Bullied Self a Letter

Most people have been bullied at some point in life. It may have been on the playground, in college or in the workplace. Think about a time you were bullied. Recall how it made you feel and write your bullied self a letter.

If someone said something that was helpful, include those words in your note to yourself. Be kind to yourself. Forgive yourself for not protecting yourself or others from bullying behaviors.

End your letter with a promise to never allow yourself or anyone else to be bullied ever again.

When You Are Finished: Fold your note and place it in an envelope that you have addressed to yourself. The next time you feel bullied, open it! Take the action that you promised yourself you would.

Write Your Workplace Policy on Bullying

Most likely, your workplace has a policy for handling bullying behaviors on the job. You probably had to read it as part of your orientation. But, do you remember what it says and does it really protect you and your co-workers?

Sit down, either alone or with your co-workers, and write the workplace policy on bullying that you *want* to have. Be sure to address the following:

- Create a clear definition of bullying. Give specific examples.

- Who should employees report to if they have concerns?

- What, if anything, should the employee attempt in order to diffuse the situation on his or her own, before involving management?

- What steps will be taken to protect the person who reports the problem?

- What specific disciplinary actions will result?

When you are finished, compare what you wrote to your actual workplace policy. If you feel your workplace policy is not doing enough to protect workers from bullying, speak to your supervisor or the human resources department about revising the policy.

Sign the Pledge!

Show your support for a Bully-Free Workplace by copying and signing the pledge on the next page. Once you sign it, post it in a place, like your break room, employee restroom or conference room.

 Make additional copies of the pledge and place them nearby with a sign urging others to join you by signing their own pledge!

The Bully-Free Workplace Pledge

Show your support for a Bully-Free Workplace by signing this pledge and committing to live by the principles described in it!

I will not:

- Gossip or spread lies about you.

- Yell at you.

- Make unfair accusations.

- Use foul language or insults.

- Insult your work habits or your personal life.

- Criticize your work or your educational background.

If I am being bullied, I will:

- Not be bullied into silence.

- Speak calmly and rationally to my bully.

- Tell the bully that the behavior is unacceptable.

- Seek help if I can't resolve the problem on my own.

- Document every incident that makes me feel uncomfortable.

If I see someone being bullied at work, I will:

- Step in and help.

- Get management or HR involved as soon as possible.

- Protect the victim, even if he or she is too afraid to seek help.

I agree with all the statements contained in this pledge. By signing below, I pledge my commitment to live by the principles described in it.

Signature _____ Date _____

Take the Next Step

Although workplace bullying is dangerous, harmful and costly, it is not illegal. Fortunately, that may not be the case much longer.

Workers' rights advocates have campaigned for years to get a law against workplace bullying. The New York state senate finally got the message and passed the Healthy Workplace Bill. The Healthy Workplace Bill is a piece of legislation that addresses the rights of all workers and would let victims of workplace bullying sue for physical, psychological or economic harm—when it results from abusive treatment on the job.

The Healthy Workplace Bill has now been introduced in more than 20 states and has been sponsored by at least 300 legislators. Discussions about a federal law were begun in 2010 with members of the U. S. House of Representatives and the U.S. Senate.

If you feel strongly about the rights of workers and would like to become part of the solution, visit:
www.healthyworkplacebill.org and click on "Take Action."

"Never be bullied into silence. Never allow yourself to be made a victim. Accept no one's definition of your life, but define yourself."
~ Harvey S. Firestone

✳ **Review What You've Learned!** ✳

- Workplace bullying is "the repeated, unreasonable actions of individuals (or groups) directed toward an employee (or a group of employees), intended to intimidate, and by doing so, creates a risk to the health and safety of the employee(s)."

- Bullying in healthcare has a long history of denial. Who wants to believe that the same people the public votes as the most "honest and ethical" professionals could or would behave in such a mean and destructive way?

- A bully usually acts out as a means to gain or retain power. Bullying usually comes from a person in a position of power (real or imagined) and involves an abuse or misuse of this power.

- Attempt to understand your bully as a frightened and fearful person who lashes out in a misguided attempt to protect herself.

- Whatever the reason for the behavior, you have the potential to turn the bully around in a peaceful, quiet and helpful way—just by reaching out.

> *"The best way to knock the chip off your neighbor's*
> *shoulder is to pat him on the back."*
> ~Author Unknown

✳ **Food for Thought** ✳

- An incident of bullying makes the news nearly every day. Do you think the general population is angrier now than they were 50 years ago? Why or why not?

- Have you ever been the victim of gossip? Do you think you handled the situation effectively?

- What consequences do you think someone should face when they are guilty of bullying a co-worker? Why?

You Can't Always Get What You Want

Everyone who works in healthcare spends a lot of time every day with people: co-workers, patients, family members, visitors and so on. Getting along with people is part of the job, but it's natural to get along better with some people than with others.

Chances are certain people rub you the wrong way. Others seem unhappy with you no matter what you do. And, still others seem to take pleasure in giving you a hard time. In return, you may feel like these people are being difficult.

What do we mean exactly when we say that someone is "difficult?" People are difficult when they get in the way of what we want or need to do. Here are a couple of examples:

Tom wants to take his lunch break just when his coworker, Sharon, asks for his help transferring a patient. Tom has transferred that particular patient by himself many times and is irritated with Sharon for needing help. He delays his lunch break long enough to help Sharon, but he's mad at her for being difficult.

Jack arrives to take over Susan's patient assignment for the evening shift. Susan tells Jack that she needs to leave work on time to pick up her daughter at school. Then, as Susan gives him report, Jack keeps asking her to clarify information and repeat lab results. Susan wishes that Jack would stop slowing her down by being difficult!

Are Sharon and Jack really difficult people? Maybe...and maybe not. It's only Tom's *opinion* that Sharon is being difficult. Maybe Tom would change his mind if he knew that Sharon is pregnant and her doctor told her not to lift patients.

And, it's Susan's *opinion* that Jack is purposely slowing her down. Would Susan think differently if she knew that, right before work, Jack learned that his father is dying? **Remember…calling someone "difficult" is a matter of opinion, not fact!**

Describing Difficult People

If you had to describe the people at work whom you believe are "difficult," would you use any of the following words? Can you think of words to add?

☐ Demanding	☐ Hostile	☐ Argumentative
☐ Irritable	☐ Uncooperative	☐ Depressed
☐ Nasty	☐ Angry	☐ Abusive
☐ Rude	☐ Complaining	☐ Scary
☐ Aggressive	☐ Ungrateful	☐ _____
☐ Critical	☐ Pushy	☐ _____
☐ Sarcastic	☐ Mean	☐ _____

Now, think about the coworkers who are *easy* to get along with. How many words can you think of to describe them?

_____

_____

_____

If you're like most people, this list will be much shorter than your first list. Why does it seem so much easier to think of the things we *don't* like about people than it is to think about the good things?

Why Are Some People Difficult?

We are all individuals...with our own personalities, likes and dislikes, personal habits and ways of communicating. Yet, some of us seem to have trouble getting along with other people. There are many reasons for this. Remember that "difficult" people may be:

- Dealing with stress or tragedy in their personal lives.

- Suffering from an illness or chronic pain.

- Dealing with a disability.

- Feeling lonely, overwhelmed or depressed.

- Wishing someone would reach out to them in kindness.

While a culture of civility starts with you, it isn't all *about* you. Remember how bullying behavior stems from a place of pain or fear? The same may be true for people who aren't bullies—but who have trouble blending with the rest of the team.

It's human nature to think that if a coworker is grumpy with you, it must be something you've done. But, chances are, it has nothing to do with you. So, don't take everything personally. For example, you always say hello to Tim when you pass him in the hallway, but he never responds. You might think to yourself, "Tim's a jerk and he hates me." But, what's the real truth? Tim is deaf in one ear and the noises in the hallway drown out your greetings.

Be Careful Calling Others Difficult

Imagine this: You've been assigned to work with a newly hired nurse, Cynthia. Your co-worker, Ted, tells you that he worked with Cynthia yesterday and she was "difficult, rude and grouchy."

So, now what? You haven't even met Cynthia, but you're already prepared for her to give you trouble. You probably wish you didn't have to work with her at all. How will this affect the way you treat Cynthia when you first meet her?

Tips for Getting Along with "Difficult" Co-Workers

Consider adjusting your attitude. If you *think* that a person is going to be difficult, he probably will be...because of the way you behave around him!

Keep your opinion to yourself. Remember, it's only your opinion that someone at work is difficult. A person who seems difficult to you may get along fine with everyone else. Or, you may get along great with a co-worker that no one else seems to like.

Ponder the problem. Try hard not to overreact when dealing with a difficult person. Ask yourself, "Is this issue really worth making a fuss about?"

Let things go. When you work with people who have given you trouble in the past, try to start fresh every day. Forget about what happened yesterday, last week or last month.

Keep your cool. If someone is yelling at you, crying or complaining loudly, try standing still, looking directly at the person...and waiting. This gives the person a chance to get all their anger out.

Don't be the "floor show." If a co-worker wants to squabble in front of the team, you might also try saying, "I want to hear everything you have to say, but not here where it might disturb others. Let's go somewhere private."

Take ten. Remember that old "rule" about counting to ten? It really does work. The next time you feel angry or upset with a coworker, breathe slowly and count to ten—before you speak. You'll feel better about the way you handle the situation.

Be the boss. Don't allow other people to control your moods. If you do, you are giving them tremendous power over you. So, if you're in a good mood, don't let someone else's grouchy attitude bring you down.

Focus on actions. When dealing with a difficult person, focus on the particular behaviors you don't like...rather than just labeling the person. For example, instead of saying to a coworker, "You're always rude to me" try saying, "I feel hurt when you don't say good morning, please or thank you to me."

Be your own cheerleader. The next time you have to work with a difficult co-worker, give yourself a little "pep talk." Tell yourself, "I'm ready for this. I can handle whatever happens today. I will not get upset, no matter what." It may seem silly, but if you start with a positive attitude (rather than telling yourself, "This is going to be awful."), your time with the person will be easier.

Play it back in your head. If you saw a videotape of yourself from a recent confrontation with a difficult person, would you be embarrassed by your own behavior? If so, how would you like to see yourself behave?

Lay on the praise. Be sure to compliment people when they behave in a positive manner. (In other words, reward the behavior you want to see them repeat.) For example, if Jane says, "Please help me get my patient to the bathroom now." instead of the grumpy way she usually says it, you might say, "Thank you for asking so nicely. I'd be happy to help you." Hopefully, she'll continue to ask nicely in the future.

Keep your word. It's always best to avoid making promises that you can't keep...but especially with "difficult" people. If you tell them you're going to do something, then do it. And, if you have to break your promise for some reason, be sure to apologize.

Watch your body language. We all want to be heard—and difficult people are no exception. If you tell co-workers that you're listening to them, but you're standing with your hands on your hips, tapping your foot and staring at a clipboard...they'll know you aren't really listening.

Know your triggers. We all have certain "pet peeves", most of which developed during our childhoods. For example, maybe your mother always nagged you to keep your hair out of your eyes. One day, a co-worker says to you, "How can you see with your hair in your eyes?" It's an innocent question, but it sets you off because you're sensitive to it. (And, you're not really mad at your co-worker, you're mad at your mother!) So, think about the little things that tend to bother you and try not to overreact when someone at work does them.

Save your strength. Don't waste your energy trying to change people who behave in a difficult manner. Instead, work on changing the way you *react* to their behavior.

Struggles, Disputes and Quarrels...Oh My!

By now, it should be clear that for an industry that requires tight teamwork, the healthcare working environment remains ripe for incivility and conflict. When you combine unrelenting stress levels, heavy workloads and the serious responsibility of caring for human lives with a fierce level of competition and a high degree of diversity, what do you get? A perfect recipe for lighting the fire, stirring the pot and brewing conflict!

Whenever people spend day after day together in the healthcare environment, conflict is unavoidable. You may be nodding in agreement or you may be thinking that you've never had a dispute with anyone. However, conflict at work happens to everyone at some point in his or her career.

Fortunately, not all conflict is bad. And with a little practice, most conflict can be avoided or resolved quickly and efficiently with very little drama!

Disagreement vs. Conflict

The start of a dispute between people usually begins with a *disagreement*. When you and a co-worker disagree, you have one opinion while your co-worker has another. Often, it doesn't really matter to either of you what the other person thinks. You both go on with your lives, each sticking to your own opinion. Usually, disagreements consist only of words and they do not affect how people interact with each other.

For example: Tim and Connie, both CNAs, disagree one day at work about the proper way to give a bath to a bedridden patient. They each express their opinion, saying it is how they were taught in school. They end the discussion by saying, "OK...you do it your way and I'll do it mine." Tim and Connie disagree, but they respect each other's opinion and have no trouble working together.

A full-blown *conflict* can begin with different opinions, but it grows into something much larger. Generally, it is not what people say, but how they *act*, that causes a disagreement to escalate into a conflict.

Conflict Equals Drama

Let's take another look at Tim and Connie's situation. Imagine that instead of agreeing to disagree about bathing a patient, they get into an ongoing struggle about who is *right*. Tim starts telling other co-workers that Connie doesn't know how to give a proper bath. Connie gives Tim hateful looks and refuses to work with him. They have entered into a contest of opposing forces. Unless their conflict is resolved, work will remain an unpleasant place for both of them!

Having gone past the point of disagreement, Tim and Connie are in a full-blown conflict, which can start causing a disruption among their co-workers and eventually affect their job performance. Tim and Connie are creating a situation where neither will back down; each thinks that they would appear to be wrong by offering a truce.

> *When the "real world" doesn't measure up to how we picture it in our minds, it can lead to pain, conflict and drama. When we resolve conflicts, we reduce the amount of drama in our lives.*

 In almost all conflicts, the problem stems not from the initial disagreement, but the way in which it is handled. A conflict can be avoided easily with the proper attitude and respect for the workplace.

What's Your Angle?

There are five main ways people deal with (or refuse to get into) conflict. Each has its advantages and disadvantages and each are appropriate in different situations.

- **Avoidance** is useful if the issue is a minor matter or if nothing is gained by entering into the conflict.

  For example, after noticing you and your supervisor chatting, a co-worker snaps, "I can't believe how much you brown-nose around here!" While her comment angers and hurts you, you decide to ignore it and go on with your day as if it did not happen.

  If there is a more serious problem than just a few harsh words, avoiding it resolves nothing—and the problem can even worsen.

- **Accommodation** relies on people giving up their own views in favor of someone else's. The accommodator is likely to take on the ideas of the other person, just to avoid sparking a confrontation.

  Let's use the same example from above. After the comment, you agree with her, saying, "Well, I want a good work evaluation this month," even though inside you don't feel that way at all.

  Generally, this method won't *solve* a problem, but it might stop a conflict in its tracks.

- **Competition** in a conflict situation arises when people with competitive attitudes take a firm stand and try to get what they want.

  Using our example: after your co-worker accuses you of brown-nosing, you snap back, "I can't believe you are listening to a private conversation. Mind your own business!"

  When both people believe they are right and are willing to fight over it, they are demonstrating a competitive attitude.

- **Collaboration** involves people trying to come to a solution that pleases everybody. It takes time because it means that each person gets to present a view and help come up with a solution.

  In our example, you might ask your co-worker to sit down with you privately so you can put yourselves in each other's shoes and find a new way to interact with each other.

  While collaboration is a great method, it is generally too time-consuming to be used for *every* workplace conflict.

- **Compromise** holds the promise of having people who disagree "meet in the middle." Each person has to give up something, but in doing so, gains something in return.

  Back to our example, you might say to your co-worker, "I don't feel I deserved that comment. First, I don't think it was brown-nosing; I like talking to our supervisor. Maybe next time we have a conversation you could join us?" By reacting with a spirit of compromise, you express your feelings in a respectful fashion. However, by inviting her to join you, you have also "given up" having a private conversation with your supervisor in the future.

Which Attitudes Do Tim and Connie Have?

Remember Tim and Connie? They are both doing their best to continue their conflict. It started as a disagreement about the best way to bathe a patient, but has turned into a contest of wills. Both feel they are right and neither will back down.

Can you guess which attitudes they are demonstrating?

Now, think about the other attitudes and why they are not being used in this situation. In other words, what are Tim and Connie *not* doing? Which of the five approaches do you think would solve the problem?

How to Wrangle a Resolution...with Civility

When conflict arises in the workplace, a simple five step process can help resolve the situation. Read through the steps to see how to easy the process can be.

1. **Realize there's a solution!** Both parties involved in the dispute need to come to the realization that the problem requires resolution. They must *agree* that the conflict needs to come to an end.

2. **Exchange viewpoints.** Perhaps the most important part of the entire process, exchanging viewpoints involves each person speaking while the other listens—so that everyone's point of view is understood. Both parties strive to remain open-minded, to speak clearly and to identify the issues.

3. **What's your problem? Mine too!** Before the process of resolution can continue, both people have to agree on their mutual problems. People tend to see things through the lens of their own personality, values, goals and prejudices. The goal of this step is to get to a *consensus* about the problems, not to force one another to see things the same way. Usually, both sides have to agree that at least one problem they share is lack of communication.

4. **Create solutions.** So that both sides feel like they are part of the solution, each should have an equal hand in negotiating a fair solution. Both should remain open to each other's ideas and really consider each proposed solution even if they have no experience with it and/or did not think of it themselves.

5. **Negotiate the fix.** The conflict is likely to be resolved at this point, at least for now. Both sides feel empathy for each other views, even if they conclude that their opinions are miles apart. The goal of this final step is to ensure that both parties have participated in and agree on a solution— and that both are happy with the outcome.

The Process in Action

Tim and Connie must put an end to their conflict, as it is hurting them both and is also causing a disruption to the rest of their team. Let's see them fix the problem by going through the five steps:

1. Connie realizes that they need to stop this fight and asks Tim politely if she can speak to him. Tim agrees and, during a break, they sit in an empty meeting room together.

2. They take turns telling one another their points of view. One speaks while the other actively listens.

3. They identify several problems: they each have a strong personality; they are competitive; and they both like to be right. Connie and Tim agree that the problem was *never* the actual bathing technique—but how they communicated with each other.

4. They discuss the bathing method they each use and decide that both techniques are acceptable and fall within the policy parameters for their workplace. However, both Tim and Connie say they will continue using their own methods. Neither person wins or loses.

5. Tim and Connie decide that, in the future, they will keep their own patient care techniques to themselves. As long as the job is getting done, they can agree to disagree on "proper" methods. If either Tim or Connie uses a method that is *not* getting the job done, they will discuss it politely at that time. In the meantime, they agree that the conflict is over—and, to enhance a culture of civility at their workplace, they both decide to apologize to their co-workers.

Does Conflict Seem to Follow You Around?

If you answered "yes" to that question, then it's YOU, not them! It's difficult to see yourself as anything but a good employee and agreeable person. Here is your rude awakening: *most* people should answer "yes" to that question. At some point, each of us has contributed to a negative work environment.

Most of us have:

- **Jumped to conclusions.** For example: Your supervisor is constantly scheduling you for days that you requested off. She tells you she has no choice. You don't believe her and become resentful toward her. (The appropriate response is to research the issue and get to the bottom of the miscommunication. But, sometimes, it seems "easier" to simply assume the worst.)

- **Disagreed with everything.** You may think this makes you assertive because you stand up for your own opinions. However, playing the "Devil's advocate" can make you come across as someone who just has to win. Try giving in on smaller issues and disputing only the larger ones. You will seem less disagreeable this way.

- **Failed to listen.** Did you know that, instead of listening to what the other person is saying, most people spend that time figuring out what they are going to say when the other person stops talking? The solution to this is to truly stop and *hear* what the other person is saying. It may save you from the stress of a full blown conflict.

- **Used hostile language.** Remember the old saying, "It's not what you say but *how* you say it."? Becoming confrontational and emotional is easy, especially for those of us with a short fuse. It's better to stay calm and deliver your words appropriately. You may even decide it's a good idea to wait until you have calmed down. And yes, sarcasm can be hostile too.

"By swallowing evil words unsaid, no one has ever harmed his stomach."

~ Winston Churchill

When It's Not You...It's Your Supervisor!

Resolving problems with a "boss" can be tricky, especially if that person has the power to make your job difficult (or make it go away).

Here are some tips for getting along with your supervisor, even if you don't always see eye to eye:

- **Review the expectations.** Make sure that your priorities match what your supervisor expects of you. You'll never measure up to your supervisor's expectations if you don't know what they are!

- **Remain professional.** Remember that you are there to provide care to your patients—not to make friends. As a professional, your goal is to get the job done and carry out your supervisor's instructions.

- **Don't expect to change others.** If you work for a "difficult" supervisor, there is probably nothing you can do to change his or her behavior. The only thing you can control is your own attitude about that person.

- **Take a look at yourself.** If a supervisor criticizes your performance, take a deep breath and look at the situation objectively. Did you really do your best? Keep in mind that constructive criticism gives us an opportunity to learn and grow professionally.

- **Keep emotions out of it.** If a supervisor confronts you about something, remain calm. If you let yourself react emotionally, the situation can turn into a "war" where you and your supervisor are fighting about who is right. Instead, simply say, "I understand. Thank you for the information." Or, try asking for advice and ideas about how your work can be improved.

- **Be careful about complaining.** It may be tempting to complain about your supervisor to your co-workers. But, be careful! You may wind up being labeled as a chronic complainer instead of a team player—and your negative comments about your supervisor may get back to him or her.

When It's Not You...It's Them!

We all know unprofessional people when we see them. Many of them go through their work day being:

- Hostile
- Rude
- Selfish
- Irresponsible
- Careless
- Tardy
- Negligent
- Uncaring

No one is perfect—and everyone has bad days now and again. But someone who is unprofessional demonstrates these negative qualities nearly every day. Here are a few tips for dealing with unprofessional co-workers:

- **Don't lose your cool.** If both of you are upset, it will only make things worse!

- **Try to work it out.** Before talking to a supervisor about the problem, sit down with your co-worker. Patiently communicate your feelings to the best of your ability.

- **You catch more flies with honey.** Have you ever heard the expression "kill them with kindness?" Try inviting the person out to lunch or to have a cup of coffee. Then, quietly discuss any misunderstandings that may have come between you.

- **Offer yourself!** If you have time, ask your co-worker if he or she needs help with anything.

- **Remain patient.** It can be extremely difficult to deal with an unprofessional co-worker. By responding in a friendly manner, the workplace (and your workday) will be much more peaceful.

"Be kind to unkind people—they need it the most."
~ Ashleigh Brilliant

Learn to Fly under the Radar

It's much easier to steer clear of conflict than it is to resolve it! Of course, you can't always stay out of it completely, but you make it much less likely to be a problem if you lay low and fly under the radar!

Here are some ways you can do that:

- **Pick your battles.** When you disagree with someone, make sure the issue is really important to you. Don't fall into the trap of continuing the argument just because you want to be "right."

- **Stay out of other people's disagreements.** If a conflict doesn't involve you directly, allow your co-workers to resolve the situation on their own.

- **Remember that people at work come from many diverse backgrounds.** Based on their culture, the way they were raised and their life experiences, they may have different views and opinions. This doesn't make them wrong—just different!

- **Separate personality from behavior.** You don't have to like each of your co-workers to get along with them. For example, you may not like Pete's boisterous personality but he's a hard worker and a real team player.

- **Always be respectful.** Keep in mind that you are in your workplace—and you need to remain calm and professional at all times (even if the other person isn't).

A workplace conflict affects more than just the people who are directly involved. If you have an ongoing "feud" with a co-worker, chances are that it is causing tension for everyone at work. Try to resolve the issue today!

What's Your Style?

Will you give in, be strong or be mean? There are three main personality styles that influence your role in a conflict: passive, assertive and aggressive. It's a good idea to be aware of your own style. Here's the breakdown:

	PASSIVE	ASSERTIVE	AGGRESSIVE
Description	You put everyone's needs first—while ignoring your own.	You stand up for your rights while showing respect for the rights of others.	You stand up for your own rights—but violate the rights of others.
How You View Your Self and Others	You may think: • *I am not important.* • *I don't matter.*	You believe: • *Everyone is important.* • *We are all equal.*	You tell others: • *Your feelings are not important.* • *You don't matter.* • *I'm superior.*
Verbal Habits and Styles	You: • Apologize frequently. • Speak in a soft or unsure voice.	You: • Use "I" statements (to take ownership of own actions). • Speak in a firm voice.	You: • Use "you" statements (to blame or accuse others). • Speak in a loud voice.
Non-Verbal Habits and Styles	You: • Avoid eye contact. • Stand with stooped shoulders.	You have: • Direct, non-threatening eye contact. • Relaxed posture.	You: • Stare with accusing eyes. • Have a tense posture, with clenched fists.
Outcomes or Results	• Low self-esteem. • Not respected by others.	• High self-esteem. • Self-respect. • Respected by others.	• Low self-esteem. • Disrespected. • Feared.

Assert Your Assertiveness

You can approach and resolve conflicts most productively when you are assertive. You might think that assertiveness comes as part of someone's personality—you're either born with it or you're not. But, even the shyest person can learn to be more assertive. It takes some work to be assertive, but it's worth the effort.

Here are some ways to work on this skill:

- **Practice!** Practice assertive communication with a friend or your spouse, in non-threatening situations. Work on getting your needs across to the other person in a way that respects both of you.

- **Nip interruptions in the bud.** Listen more than you speak and allow the other person to finish his or her thought before your respond.

- **Avoid hurting others.** If you question how your communication might be understood, ask yourself: "Would I feel comfortable if someone were talking to me this way?"

- **Treat everyone with kindness and respect.** Being assertive is a lot like following the Golden Rule. Behave with courtesy and respect toward everyone—from the maintenance man to the "head honcho" of your organization.

If You're Really Good at This...

Think you might have what it takes to help others manage and resolve conflict in your workplace? Did you know that large companies, in all industries including healthcare, utilize certified experts (called *Workplace Mediation Specialists*) to help handle conflicts in the workplace.

A Workplace Mediation Specialist does not need any particular degree, only a history of working in your field is important. Certification can be obtained through seminars, webinars and continuing education courses. Go to www.mediationworks.com to find out what one company has to offer. Talk to your supervisor about opportunities at you workplace!

KEEP WORKING ON IT!
Practice Using "I" Statements

The best way to discuss a problem is to avoid personal attacks, dramatic statements and blame. If you talk about how you *feel*—rather than pointing a finger at the other person—you are less likely to put the other person on the defensive.

Remember, when assertive people use "I" statements, they own up to their own actions. Try your hand at turning these accusatory "you" statements into less threatening "I" statements.

IT'S YOU!	NO, IT'S ME!
Example: *You are so mean to me.*	*I feel hurt when you raise your voice at me.*
1. You don't work as hard as I do.	I feel. . .
2. You ask for help too often.	I feel. . .
3. You get all the easy patients.	I feel. . .
4. You take too many days off.	I feel. . .
5. You act like you're better than me.	I feel. . .
6. You never thank me when I help you.	I feel. . .
7. You are really grouchy.	I feel. . .
8. You ignore me all the time.	I feel. . .
9. You never help me when I ask you.	I feel. . .
10. You started it.	I feel. . .

KEEP WORKING ON IT!
Practice Active Listening

Listening is an active process, like driving or paying bills. To do it right, you have to really focus on the task, understand what's important and make critical decisions on what to do next. Active listening includes:

- **Hearing.** Hearing means listening enough to catch what is being said. For example, say you are listening to an inservice on IV pumps. You hear the speaker mention that there is an emergency shut-off key behind a secret door in the back. If you can repeat this fact when the program is over, then you heard what was said.

- **Understanding.** The next part of listening happens when you take what you have heard and understand it in your own way. Let's go back to the IV pump. Perhaps, after you heard the information about the secret door, you think you should probably check it out yourself. You inspect the demo model and find the door. You open it and see the key.

- **Judging.** After you are sure you understand what the speaker has said, you can judge for yourself whether the information is important and if any action should be taken. In this case, an appropriate action might be to remember this information in case you need it in the future!

What's Stopping You?

What's the hardest part about active listening for you? For example, maybe *hearing* is a problem because you become bored and think about all the other things you could be doing. Or maybe *understanding* is a problem because you have trouble figuring out what others really mean.

If hearing is a problem, you may want to practice forcing yourself to listen when people talk. For example, your supervisor says, "I need you go down to the storage room, take inventory, make a list of all the items we need and then call in the order to the supply company." But, you zone out halfway through the instructions and miss the part about placing the order. This means you have not heard a major part of what has been delegated to you.

If understanding is a problem, try repeating the information back to the speaker to clarify. You might say, "Okay, so I need to take an inventory, make a list and then place the order. Is that right?"

Quick Tips for Being a Good Listener

- **Give your full attention to the speaker**, not to what else is going on in the room.

- **Be quiet.** Let others finish before you start talking.

- **Don't get ahead of yourself.** Listen completely before you begin to think about what you want to say next.

- **Ask questions.** If you are not sure you understand, just ask.

- **Listen with your face.** Make eye contact, nod, smile, frown, laugh or be silent to let the speaker know that you are really listening.

Now, Try It Yourself!

Without telling anyone what you are doing, practice active listening during your next conversation.

When the conversation is over, write down the main points you "heard" the person say. Then, write your "understanding" of those points. Finally, "judge" for yourself if the information is important and if any action should be taken.

Once you have written everything down, explain to the person you were talking with that you are practicing "active listening."

Show the person what you heard and understood. *Make sure it is correct!* If not, keep practicing.

Practice Resolving Conflict

Do you have an ongoing conflict with a co-worker or supervisor? If so, use the following steps to begin to resolve the conflict today! Here's how:

Realize there's a solution. Stop avoiding or escalating the issue right away. Understand that the conflict has a solution and needs to be discussed as soon as possible.

Who are you having a conflict with? _____

Exchange viewpoints. Clearly define your side of the problem.

_____

_____

Now, listen and understand the *other* person's side of the problem. Put the other person's problem into words to clarify it for yourself.

_____

_____

Create solutions. Have each person list two or three creative solutions to this problem.

_____

_____

Negotiate the fix. Decide on the best solution together. How will you resolve this conflict today?

_____

_____

✳ **Review What You've Learned!** ✳

- A full-blown conflict can begin with different opinions, but it grows into something much larger. Generally, it is not what people say, but how they *act*, that causes a disagreement to escalate into a conflict.

- There are five main ways people deal with (or refuse to deal with) conflict. They are avoidance, accommodation, competition, collaboration and compromise. Each has its advantages and disadvantages and each are appropriate in different situations.

- Listening is an active process, like driving or paying bills. To do it right, you have to really focus on the task, understand what's important and make critical decisions on what to do next.

- It's much easier to avoid conflict than it is to resolve it! Of course, you can't always avoid it completely, but you make it much less likely to be a problem if you lay low and fly under the radar!

"When you are confronted with an opponent, conquer him with love."
~Gandhi

✳ **Food for Thought** ✳

- In general, when two people have a disagreement at work, do you think that *one* person is mostly to blame? Why or why not?

- Do you think that most workplace conflicts start over little things or big things? Why?

- During an average workday, which do you do more of: listening or talking? How does this affect your healthcare team?

- Think of one difficult person at work. What would you like to have from him or her? Have you ever asked this person for what you want? Why or why not?

Taking It to the Extreme

Rolling your eyes at someone, participating in gossip, disagreeing for the fun of it, snapping at a co-worker...these are all examples of less than professional behavior. If they happen repeatedly or are always directed at the same person, they would probably be considered bullying. As you've read (and perhaps even experienced), working in a culture that allows these incivilities wears you down and puts you at risk for burnout.

Sometimes, unprofessional behavior in the workplace goes beyond "passive" bullying and moves into the far more serious territory of workplace violence. For example, you may encounter a co-worker for whom anger is a way of life—and his or her actions could be a threat to your health and well-being.

The Consequences of Anger

Anger is one letter short of danger.
~Eleanor Roosevelt

Not worried about anger issues at your workplace? **Consider these statistics:**

- Nearly half of all workers admit to losing their temper on the job.

- Thirty eight percent of men report being unhappy at work.

- Nearly 30 percent of nurses have been attacked at work.

- Up to 60 percent of all absences from work are caused by stress.

- One in 20 of us has had a fight with a co-worker.

- Every day in the United States, 65 people are killed and more than 6,000 are wounded in interpersonal violence.

What Makes People Angry?

Anger arises in different people for various reasons and is usually linked to a past experience or a build-up of frustration.

Past Experience: A person who was abused as a child may become angry when she hears someone else being yelled at. Or, a person who has been teased or bullied may get angry if he hears people teasing someone else.

Frustration Level: A person's tolerance for frustration can decrease when there is stress or anxiety, physical or emotional pain, drugs or alcohol or even from the pressure of having a bad day.

The most common factors that make people angry are:

- Grief, losing a loved one
- Rudeness
- Fatigue
- Hunger
- Pain
- Withdrawal from drugs or certain medications
- Some physical conditions, such as pre-menstrual syndrome
- Physical or mental illness
- Alcohol abuse, drug abuse
- Injustice
- Being teased or bullied

- Humiliation
- Embarrassment
- Deadlines
- Traffic jams
- Disappointment
- Sexual frustration
- Sloppy service
- Failure
- Infidelity
- Burglary
- Financial problems

In general, people get angry when they feel that they are being *threatened*. The threat may be a real or imagined danger to themselves, their ego or someone they love or care for.

The Biology of Anger

Anger affects the whole body because it triggers the "fight or flight" response. This is the primitive, automatic response which prepares our bodies to "fight" or "flee" from an attack, harm or threat to our survival.

Stemming from an area of the brain called the hypothalamus, the "fight or flight" response initiates a sequential release of hormones, including adrenaline, noradrenaline and cortisol.

This sudden flood of hormones causes the following changes in the body:

Your **brain** has trouble focusing on small tasks.

Your **pupils** enlarge to allow in as much light as possible.

Heart rate and **blood pressure** increase.

The **blood glucose level** increases.

Your **muscles** contract and **veins** constrict leading to those "chill" and "goose bumps" you may develop.

To save energy for emergency use, your **digestion** and **immune systems** shut down.

The goal of these physical responses is to help you survive a dangerous situation by preparing you to either *run* for your life or *fight* for your life. Is it any wonder that anger takes a toll on the body and the mind?

Are You Willing to Pay the Price?

People who have a hard time controlling their anger in the workplace risk losing their co-workers' respect and, ultimately, their jobs. But, even worse, they risk losing their health. *Chronic anger can cause physical health problems, such as:*

- Backache

- Headaches

- Hypertension

- Insomnia

- Irritable bowel syndrome

- Skin disorders

- Stroke

- Heart attack

- Lower pain threshold

- Weakened immune system

In addition, chronic anger can lead to emotional problems, including:

- Depression

- Eating disorders

- Alcohol abuse

- Drug abuse

- Self-injury

- Low self-esteem

- Moodiness

When Anger Becomes a Problem

Obviously, anger itself is not always bad. In fact, experts say anger is a natural emotion that is important for survival. That's why the "fight or flight" response is programmed into our DNA.

It is *uncontrolled* anger that takes incivility to the extreme, making it a problem with the potential for severe consequences.

So how can you tell if your own (or someone else's) anger poses a problem?

Here are some clues:

- The anger leads to trouble with the law.

- There are constant arguments especially between partners, parents, children or co-workers.

- Arguments lead to physical fights.

- Someone gets hit.

- There are threats of violence to people or property.

- Emotional outbursts occur even when *minor* things go wrong.

Keeping Your Cool in the Moment

"Before you give someone a piece of your mind,
make sure you can get by with what is left."
~ Author Unknown

If you catch yourself ready to "have it out" with a co-worker, *embrace civility* instead by practicing the following tips:

Call a "Time Out." Before you say or do something you will regret, say, *"I need to take a time-out."* Then walk away from the situation, take a deep breath and count to 10. Use this time to think about what you want to say. Return only when you feel calm and in control.

Get your finger on the "Edit" button. In the heat of the moment, it's easy to say something you'll regret later. By taking a minute to collect your thoughts before saying anything, you'll be able to press that edit button *before* the thoughts become words.

Express yourself. Once you're thinking clearly, express your needs and concerns in a calm and rational way. Speak clearly and directly, without hurting others or trying to control them.

Use "I" statements. Remember how starting a sentence with "I" (instead of "you") avoids criticizing or placing blame on others? For example, say *"I feel really embarrassed about this mistake"* instead of, *"You made a horrible mistake that makes us all look bad."*

Find the humor. Lightening up the mood can help diffuse any tension between you and your co-workers. Don't use sarcasm, though. It can hurt feelings and make things worse.

Identify possible solutions. Remind yourself that anger doesn't fix anything—it throws up unnecessary roadblocks. So, instead of focusing on what made you mad, work on resolving the issue at hand. For example, if your co-worker's sloppiness makes your job harder, try your hand at designing an organizational system that provides a place for everything.

Don't hold a grudge. Forgiveness is a powerful tool. If you allow anger and other negative feelings to crowd out positive emotions, you might find yourself swallowed up by your own bitterness or sense of injustice. If you can forgive the person who angered you, you might both learn from the situation.

Make a plan. As soon as you no longer feel angry, review how you handled the situation. Then, plan a relaxation ritual you can practice the *next* time angry feelings surface. It can be deep-breathing exercises, imagining a relaxing scene or repeating a calming word or phrase, such as, "Take it easy."

Write it down. Take a moment to jot down your plan for soothing your soul next time something—or someone—gets your dander up. Decide on (at least) three actions you can take next time you feel yourself boiling over...and promise yourself that you'll follow through.

A PROMISE TO MYSELF

The next time I become angry at work, I will do the following:

1. _____

2. _____

3. _____

"I don't have to attend every argument I'm invited to."
~Author Unknown

What Lights Your Fuse?

If you know you have trouble controlling your anger, focus on the specific things that irritate you. By honing in on what triggers your anger, you may find it easier to steer clear of those situations before a problem emerges—or at least make better choices in the heat of the moment.

Identify your anger triggers. On a separate sheet of paper, list all the things that make you angry, especially when you are at work.

For example, maybe you become angry when co-workers don't complete all their own tasks and leave the work for you. Or, perhaps you get mad when you see others gossiping or backstabbing. Does your supervisor's management style tick you off? Put it on the list.

Decide what you will do. Once you know your anger triggers, think of a few things you can do for each situation to keep your anger under control.

For example, if you said that gossiping co-workers make you angry, you might list: "Count to ten; breathe deeply; walk away; and then, calmly return to express my feelings in a non-threatening way."

Practice assertive communication. Train yourself to express your feelings and needs *assertively* when you feel angry or frustrated. Assertiveness has nothing to do with aggressiveness. Assertiveness includes respect for yourself *and* others.

Managing Anger on a Deeper Level

Is your anger a chronic condition that rears its ugly head way more often than you'd like? To begin the process of reining in your anger, try incorporating some of the following suggestions into your daily routine:

Exercise your breath. Being able to control your breath is one of the most powerful tools against anger. Here's how: Take *a deep breath in through your nose* for six seconds. *Hold your breath* for two seconds. *Breathe out through your mouth* for eight seconds. Repeat the process five times. As you breathe in, your belly should inflate like a balloon. As you exhale, your belly should collapse or be pulled in toward your spine. Your goal is to push out all the stale, "angry" air in your lungs.

Let nature empower you. Take a walk outside. Notice the trees, the clouds, the plants and the birds. Experts agree that just twenty minutes spent in a natural environment has the power to restore and refresh the mind. Whether it's your back yard, a local park or even an outdoor courtyard at your workplace, being surrounded by Mother Nature decreases anger, while boosting vitality, energy, mood and happiness. (Performing your breathing exercise while you enjoy the outdoors *doubles* the benefit!)

Stretch out your anger. Your muscles become tense when you are angry. It's part of that "fight or flight" response. When your muscles are tensed and you're ready to strike, your mind goes blank. Stretching unlocks any stiff muscles and improves oxygen flow to the brain, allowing you to think more clearly.

Eat, sleep and exercise. Studies show that individuals who exercise at least twenty minutes per day, sleep a minimum of seven hours per night and eat healthy foods have fewer feelings of anger and irritation—plus higher levels of happiness and well-being. So, take the advice that you've probably given to countless patients—renew your body and spirit with the right foods, plenty of sleep and regular exercise.

Tell yourself what you need to hear. Talking to yourself in an understanding, calming manner is another way to keep from making poor choices while you are angry. When you begin to feel angry, tell yourself something like, *"I'm supposed to learn something from this situation. I may not know what that is right now, and that's okay. The calmer I stay, the more likely I can continue making good decisions. I am a good person and I have nothing to be ashamed of."*

Don't bottle-up your feelings. Controlling your anger does not mean you become passive and ignore your feelings. It means you know how to get a hold of your emotions and express yourself calmly and rationally. When it's safe to do so, talk about why you are angry. Remember, to speak with assertiveness and identify what you need in a non-threatening way. This is much better than sitting on your anger and it's more constructive than exploding in a rage which can spiral out of control.

Keep a journal. Keep a notebook handy that you can pull out and write down your frustrations, irritations and annoyances. What is making you mad, and why? Don't edit your feelings here...you can say what you want without any consequences. The goal is to dump your anger out onto the paper, privately, and then let the anger go.

Look on the bright side. After writing your angry feelings in your journal, end by listing five things you are grateful for in your life. Then, end each day by listing a few things you are grateful for, just before you go to sleep.

Pray. If you are religious or spiritual, it can be helpful to pray for peacefulness and patience. Avoid asking for physical things, like more money or a better job. Instead focus on finding some peace in your mind. The rest will fall into place.

Do "The Change Up." Remember the movies, "Freaky Friday" and "The Change Up"? The characters in these movies got the opportunity to change places with someone else. Imagine doing the same thing when you are angry with a co-worker. Put yourself in their shoes and try to see the world from their vantage point. This is known as empathy...and the more you practice it, the less intense your anger will become.

Be kind to yourself. Treat yourself with the same kindness, compassion and civility that you extend to your patients or loved ones. When you do this, you will dampen any anger you feel toward yourself when/if you make a mistake. While it might seem silly, try speaking gently to yourself—as if you were a three-year-old child. You may find it helps you to take responsibility for your part in the problem while still being able to bounce back and move forward.

Turn your anger into action. There are many injustices in the world that cause people to feel angry and helpless. Instead of complaining and stewing about them, do something to make your world better! Improve your workplace with a new idea. Enrich your family and finances by adding to your education. Help the community by volunteering to feed the hungry, clean your neighborhood, fight crime or care for children. When you see a problem, don't waste time getting angry...just get busy!

Know when to seek help. Controlling chronic anger can be a challenge. You can't just wish it away. If your anger seems out of control, causes you to do things you regret or hurts those around you, embrace civility for *yourself* and seek professional help. There are proven programs, methods and counseling therapies that can help!

Dana's Story

"It is wise to direct your anger towards problems - not people;
to focus your energies on answers - not excuses."
~ William Arthur Ward

Dana worked at a long term care facility. She found the environment stressful because policies and procedures changed constantly and the facility suffered from a high employee turnover rate. She had too many patients and not enough time to devote to each one. Dana lost her temper often and became very angry and impatient, especially towards her co-workers.

Dana believed that people were taking advantage of her and that the only way she could get them to listen was to "get in their faces" and be aggressive. As a result, her relationships with co-workers deteriorated steadily and most staff members avoided working with her whenever possible. Several co-workers complained to the supervisor, saying that Dana was responsible for feeding the culture of incivility at the facility.

The less her team members interacted with her, the angrier she became...and so it went, a vicious downward spiral. Finally, her supervisor, Martin, decided that if Dana failed to manage her anger, the company would have to let her go. After talking it through with her, Martin encouraged Dana to speak to a counselor specializing in anger management. Martin also recommended contacting the company's employee assistance program (EAP) for a referral. He explained that the goal of their EAP was to help employees deal with personal problems that were adversely impacting their work performance, health or well-being. Martin assured Dana that the EAP maintained complete confidentiality.

Dana took her supervisor's advice and, with the help of the EAP, made an appointment with a therapist. They met six times over the next six weeks to explore the issues behind Dana's anger. They also discussed appropriate ways to manage and express frustrations, how to use relaxation techniques and how to develop assertiveness skills to help Dana communicate her feelings.

Dana made good progress, and soon felt more relaxed and better able to control her anger at work and at home. Her relationships with co-workers improved and she began a civil dialogue with her supervisor—offering her help and suggestions for resolving workplace difficulties.

Where to Look for Help

If your issues with anger go beyond having a short fuse once in a while, consider these alternatives:

- Request a referral from your doctor to a counselor who specializes in anger management.

- Ask family members, friends or other trusted personal contacts for their recommendations.

- Your health insurer, employee assistance program (EAP), clergy, or state or local agencies might offer additional recommendations.

Do you want more information? If you would like to learn more about anger management—or you'd like some help but aren't ready to speak to someone face-to-face, check out these online anger management resources:

- For general information about anger management or to attend an online learning session, check out **Anger Management Online**: http://angermanagementonline.com

- On the website for the **American Psychological Association**, there is a helpful report called "Controlling Anger—Before It Controls You." It is available in both English and Spanish. www.apa.org/topics/anger/control.aspx

- The **Get the Angries Out** website offers practical anger management advice for adults, children, couples, teachers and more. You can sign up to receive a free newsletter, if desired. www.angriesout.com

"Anger, in general, is healthy. Just like sadness or happiness, it's a normal emotion. Where people get into trouble is when anger becomes a behavior that is physically, verbally or emotionally inappropriate."
~ Carole D. Stovall

When Extreme Incivility Turns Violent

There is no denying the threat of workplace violence for healthcare workers. In fact, our industry involves nearly *half* of the total injuries caused by workplace violence across the U.S. Sadly, nursing assistants who work in long-term care facilities have the highest incidence of workplace violence of *all* American workers.

Every year, just under 1000 people die in America as a result of workplace violence. Hundreds of thousands are injured every year as a result of workplace aggression. While these statistics are shocking, they don't represent the true picture—because many cases of workplace violence are *never even reported.*

There is a dangerous myth among healthcare workers; many believe workplace violence is "just part of the job." Getting hit, pinched, slapped, yelled at or threatened is <u>not</u> okay in any situation and is especially not okay while you are at work.

Workplace violence is defined as "verbal threats and physical assaults occurring to workers while on duty," and can be committed by co-workers, patients, family members, strangers or even someone you personally know and love.

What Is Considered Workplace Violence?

- **Verbal harassment** can come from co-workers or patients and should always be reported to management. It includes name calling, humiliation, criticism or inappropriate sexual remarks.

- A **verbal threat** is when someone actually *says* they are going to harm you (or someone else) in some way. They may tell you what they would like to do or how they would like to do it, or they may just make statements like, *"I'm going to get you,"* or *"Watch your back."*

  If you hear someone being threatened or are the victim of a verbal threat, tell your supervisor immediately. Don't place yourself in the position of trying to *decide* if the person will actually follow through and cause harm. Assume the person means to follow through and take action to protect yourself and others.

- **Disorderly conduct** can be defined as any disruptive behavior such as fighting, yelling or throwing things—and continuing to do so after being asked to stop. This type of behavior can cause you (and others) to feel unsafe and may actually lead to physical harm.

  Do not attempt to stop the person yourself. Get yourself and others out of harm's way and call for help immediately. If you work in a place that has security on site, call for a security officer. If you are in a patient's home or security is unavailable, call 911.

- **Slander** is when someone intends to harm the character, reputation or career of another person. Usually, it involves a false statement of fact about a person to someone else that causes actual harm. In the workplace, this may be done by current or former co-workers.

  Just to clarify: name calling, spreading rumors, gossiping and expressing personal opinions are usually not considered slander *unless* they lead to harm or cause someone to get fired for something that is untrue.

- **Attempts to cause physical harm** are another form of workplace violence. Let's say that your co-worker's husband shows up and angrily demands to see his wife. When you tell him that you don't know where she is, he grabs a clipboard and throws it at you. You duck and it misses. You know this guy tends to be a "hot head", so no harm done, right? Wrong. This is an attempt to cause you physical harm and needs to be reported.

  Even if the attempt is unsuccessful, you must report any attempts to cause physical harm in order to protect yourself and others from potential future harm. The next time someone throws something, you may not be so lucky.

- **Actual physical harm** can be the result of intentional grabbing, pinching, scratching, slapping, punching, thrown objects or burns—which are all reportable offenses. This is not *just part of the job.*

  Notify your supervisor and seek treatment immediately for bruises, breaks in the skin, blows to the head or other trauma.

While some of the violence at healthcare workplaces is caused by patients, their family members or strangers, there are many violent acts, including murder, committed by either current or past employees. With employee violence, there are usually warning signs that the person is unstable or capable of committing a violent act. That's why it is crucial to report a co-worker's angry or hostile behavior to your supervisor and/or the authorities. You may be witnessing only the beginning—and by reporting it, you might stop the violence in its tracks and get the employee some much needed help.

When Someone Else is Angry

Watch out for these warning signs that a co-worker is angry:

- Yelling, swearing and making threats.
- Looking flushed and tense, with clenched fists.
- Speaking or breathing too fast.
- Glaring intensely.
- Standing too close to others.
- Pacing or stamping their feet.
- Throwing objects.

What to Do If You Feel Threatened

If you are confronted by an aggressive co-worker who is taking incivility to the extreme, forget about resolving the situation yourself. Instead, remain calm, trust your instincts and protect your personal safety by following these three guidelines:

FIRST: Quickly and calmly end the interaction without making the situation worse.

- You can do this by telling the person you will not accept abusive treatment. Avoid touching the angry person unless you know from past experience that touching him or her is safe.
- Be a good role model and stay calm. If you get upset, the aggressive person may become more violent.
- Stand at least an arm's length away from an enraged person. Avoid letting the person trap you in a corner or block your exit from the room.

- If the behavior continues, ask the person to leave—or leave yourself.

- Tell other staff members and have them leave the immediate area as well.

SECOND: Get help!

- Send for security or call 911. Inform your supervisor of the situation.

- If you have threatened to call the police or security, you must follow through—even if the co-worker is someone you have known for years.

THIRD: File an incident report.

- Remember, if it is not documented, it didn't happen.

- Don't allow abusive co-workers to get away with threatening or hurting you.

- Do your part to end the violence against healthcare workers.

The Broken Windows Theory

Originally, the "Broken Windows" theory pertained to crime that occurred in neighborhoods. According to the theory, if people in a community accepted "minor" crimes (like broken windows) without reporting them, the perpetrators would slowly "up the ante" by committing more serious crimes. Why should they stop their illegal activities if no one took a stand against them?

Let's apply the same theory to the workplace. If people accept a low level of incivility or workplace violence (such as verbal bullying or intimidation) and fail to report it, bullies will slowly *escalate* their inappropriate behavior. Over time, their actions may become increasingly aggressive—leading to more serious consequences for the victims.

Remember the dangerous myth: *"It's just part of the job."* This myth leads to many cases of workplace violence going *unreported.* The silence of *failing to report* is interpreted as *acceptance* by the criminals who commit aggressive acts.

 Frequently, offenders do not fear getting into trouble for their incivility, even if it is extreme—*because they are sure you won't tell.* **Prove them wrong by embracing an attitude of zero-tolerance toward incivility of any kind.**

✳ **Review What You've Learned!** ✳

- Anger is a natural emotion important for survival. However, uncontrolled anger takes incivility to the extreme, making it a problem with the potential for severe consequences.

- Controlling chronic anger can be a challenge. You can't just wish it away. There are proven anger management programs, methods and counseling therapies that can help.

- Workplace violence is defined as "verbal threats and physical assaults occurring to workers while on duty," and can be committed by co-workers, patients, family members, strangers or even someone you personally know and love.

- It is crucial to report a co-worker's angry or hostile behavior. You may be witnessing only the beginning—and by reporting it, you might stop violence in its tracks and get the employee some much needed help.

"The quality of our lives is about treating each other well in every situation.
We are all the trustees of one another's happiness and well-being in life."
~ Dr. P. M. Forni

✳ **Food for Thought** ✳

- What role does the media play in encouraging or discouraging anger? For example, do you think watching people get angry and even say hurtful things to each other on reality television shows leads to more anger and incivility in those who are watching?

- Many times, when employees feel threatened on the job, they will simply quit and look for another job, while the person or situation that is causing fear stays behind to torment others. What could be done to break this cycle?

9 Paving the Path to Civility

"Ok, great," you're thinking. "I've read the whole book. Now I can practice self-awareness, manage my moods, build professional relationships, live and work with integrity, battle bullies, work well with a team, manage conflict and put a lid on anger!" Yet, it feels like something is missing—and it is.

The information contained in previous chapters can help you tweak your own attitude, embrace civility and enrich your relationships with co-workers. But, what about the problems with "the system" that help create stress and lead to a culture of incivility in the first place?

Working in healthcare, you still face unsafe staffing ratios, grueling working conditions, sicker and more demanding patients, pressure to stay abreast of ever-changing technology and the nagging feeling that you are merely a replaceable part in a giant machine.

Civility expert, Dr. P. M. Forni, author of *The Civility Solution: What to Do When People Are Rude* writes, "Incivility often occurs when people are stressed, unhappy, and rushed." Sound familiar? You (and your co-workers) probably spend a good portion of your workday feeling stressed, unhappy and rushed. It's no wonder the collective civility of the team is compromised. Of course, this does not excuse anyone's bad behavior. Rather, it gives some insight into the root of the problem.

So, now it's time to identify the *specific* reasons you and your co-workers are stressed, unhappy and rushed—and to do something about them.

For example, maybe you are feeling stressed because your team is constantly understaffed. Maybe there are other safety issues that are not being addressed.

Perhaps your supervisor is frustrated and unhappy because she feels like she has no control over her budget or key policies and procedures. Your co-worker may feel rushed because another shift left her with extra work.

The path toward civility is paved with solutions
to all the problems that make you and your co-workers
feel stressed, unhappy and rushed.

Get Down to Business

The final exercise in this book might turn into your life's most important work. This is your "Pay It Forward" moment—where you figure out what needs to be done to make your workplace a happier and more civil place than it was when you first arrived.

"Only those who will risk going too far can possibly
find out how far one can go."
~ T. S. Elliot

So, take a moment and reflect on everything you've learned. Curl up in a comfy chair and sip a cup of tea (or a glass of wine). Light a candle, if you are so inclined. Breathe. Get quiet with yourself and your soul.

Feel the power you hold as a healthcare employee.

- You have power in numbers. *Healthcare workers make up the largest group of employees in a single industry.* This alone gives you enough power to make changes.

- You have "expert power." You know what you are talking about!

- And finally, there is power in the trust, respect and admiration bestowed upon you by the public.

Take your power, harness it, train it, and most importantly,
USE IT to make positive changes in healthcare!

Will You Stay Put or Run for the Hills?

Age wrinkles the body. Quitting wrinkles the soul."
~ Douglas MacArthur

According to expert estimates, nearly one fifth of all healthcare workers who provide direct care to patients will leave their profession within the first three years of working. But, why are they leaving?

Healthcare workers abandon the profession for many reasons. Some seek early retirement; others cite home and family obligations. But, one study revealed the following top four reasons (in descending order) for leaving healthcare:

- **Burnout** or **stressful work environments**

- The **physical demands** of the job

- Inadequate **staffing**

- Inconvenient **scheduling**

Heather, an RN in Maryland, faced these exact issues:

"I always knew I wanted to be a nurse. I wanted to care for people. It seemed like a very admirable job. I went to an orientation at the college where they talked about the nursing shortage, job security and the higher than average wages—and I felt like it was a win-win situation. The nursing workforce would get another nurse...and I would get to BE that nurse! I enrolled in the program, and within three years, I graduated with honors and got my first job."

"The hospital had a great orientation planned. My first three weeks were spent in the classroom. After that, I was scheduled to work side-by-side with an experienced nurse for three full weeks. Unfortunately, because of staffing shortages, after only three days, I was asked to jump right in and start taking my own patient assignment."

"I was in an unfamiliar place and under a tremendous amount of stress. I couldn't find supplies when I needed them. When I asked the charge nurse for help with a difficult patient, I was told, 'Sink or swim, girl. This is what you went to school for.' When I had to stay late to finish my charting, my supervisor told me there was no room in the budget for overtime and that I'd have to clock out and finish my paperwork on my own time."

"After 3 twelve hour shifts in a row, I felt like a zombie."

Getting Stuck in the Mud

On her first day off after those three long workdays, Heather slept! When she awoke, she was mad. She felt lied to, used and taken advantage of. She was exhausted, discouraged and disillusioned. She dreaded returning to work and seriously considered quitting her job immediately.

Then reality snuck in and Heather remembered she had a car payment, student loans and rent to pay. She thought about all the time and energy she'd invested in nursing school. And, she recalled all the reasons she wanted to become a nurse in the first place. The bottom line: she wanted to *care* for people. So, Heather went back.

Day after day, month after month, Heather *kept* going back—even though the situation only worsened. Over time, Heather's workload got heavier and heavier. And, every time she mastered a skill, she found herself assigned to patients who required even more complicated care.

To make matters worse, Heather landed in the middle of another problem that impacted her daily work. It seemed the nursing team became embroiled in a petty exchange of intimidation and sabotage with the nursing assistant staff. Initially, Heather was unaware of the hostilities, but she soon became a casualty of the conflict.

One day, Heather asked her nursing assistant for a blood sugar reading on a patient. The nursing assistant replied, "Yeah, I'll put it in the computer in a minute." Heather said, "If you have the reading, can you just tell me now so I can prepare the patient's medication?" The nursing assistant sighed and rolled her eyes. She found the reading and grudgingly relayed it to Heather. From then on, she began to ignore Heather and even refused to answer questions when asked. She mocked Heather to other staff members and nicknamed her "Hurry-Up Heather."

A few weeks later, Heather entered one of her patient's rooms and found the woman naked and covered in blood and urine. The patient suffered from delirium and had yanked out her own IV and catheter. Heather could hear the nursing assistant laughing in the hall with another staff member. She said, "I saw that woman going crazy in there, but I was not about to help one of Hurry-Up Heather's patients!"

Each day brought new anxiety and added stress. Then one day, Heather hurt her back helping a patient who had fallen. When she went to her supervisor to report the injury, she was told it was her own fault for not following the "no lift" rules. Heather was ready to call it quits.

> *"Sometimes courage is the quiet voice at the end of the day*
> *saying, 'I will try again tomorrow."*
> ~ Mary Anne Radmacher

What Should Heather Do?

All the problems facing Heather may seem overwhelming. Fortunately, none of the issues are impossible to resolve. All it takes is a little bit of time, energy, determination and some leadership skills.

First, Heather sat down and made a list of her top three concerns. It looked like this:

- **We are short staffed constantly.** This means I am caring for too many patients and don't have enough time to give proper care to anyone.

- **My orientation was cut short.** I don't feel I was properly trained. New nurses on the unit say the same thing. Our unit is full of people who have not been adequately trained.

- **Everyone is so mean to one another.** I really believe that if we were kinder to each other, we could find a way to overcome the other challenges.

So, how do you fix problems like these?

Heather attacked her issues one at a time. She joined a professional campaign to insist lawmakers pass safer staffing laws. As of this writing, *15 states and the District of Columbia have enacted legislation and/or adopted regulations addressing nurse staffing.*

These laws might never pass unless healthcare workers like you get involved.

Join a Professional Organization

 Like Heather, you may want to get involved in making positive changes at the local, state or federal levels of government. If so, consider joining a professional organization representing your occupation. There are professional organizations for nurses, nurse practitioners, nursing assistants, physical, occupational, and speech therapists, doctors, researchers, billers and coders, administrative assistants, managers and administrators.

Professional associations have the resources and strategies to bring your voice to the policy makers. In addition, professional organizations monitor public policy and provide their members with reliable information related to policy issues and policy makers.

The Next Step

To address the problem of orientation, Heather got involved in education services and volunteered to be a mentor to newly hired employees. Once she was comfortable in that role, she collaborated with the Staff Development Educators to create a program for training preceptors. That meant that each new recruit would have a specially trained mentor serving as a "partner" during orientation.

Explore Shared Governance

If you'd like to become involved in making changes within your institution, find out if your employer offers a Shared Governance program. Shared Governance is a way to empower every member of the healthcare team to influence decision-making. It makes every employee part "manager" with a personal stake in the success of the organization.

Shared Governance is not a new idea. It emerged about 40 years ago in response to an earlier nursing shortage. However, it has recently regained momentum again because it became one of the expectations of the American Nurses Credentialing Center's Magnet Recognition Program.

If your workplace does not already have a "Shared Governance" program, talk to your supervisors about starting one today! Get more information at www.sharedgovernance.org.

Heather's Civility Squad

Heather was stumped by the civility problem. She could see that getting laws passed for issues like safe staffing ratios could lead to less stress for healthcare workers. And, less stress may mean less incivility—but not necessarily.

After all, you can't just write a law and *force* people to be nice to each other. Furthermore, there is no "one-size-fits-all" solution. In any given workplace, the dynamics of incivility are as varied as the individuals who are involved. Heather's third problem, reversing the culture of incivility, was much harder to fix.

One day at work, Heather was discussing the issue with a trusted fellow nurse. A nursing assistant overheard the conversation and joined in. They realized they were each facing the same issues—and these issues were all underlined by incivility. The small group decided to meet again for lunch a week later—and it was then that their solution was born. They decided to create a team they called the "Civility Squad."

Here's what they did:

First, they started talking to other co-workers about their idea. After a few weeks, they had assembled a diverse team with members representing every level of staff. They decided they should meet at least once a month. They weren't completely sure what they would *do*, but at least they were committed to sitting down to discuss the issues.

At their first meeting, they wrote their mission statement. It read, *"We value the efforts of every individual employee, regardless of rank or position, and we appreciate their contributions to the team. We are committed to treating each of our colleagues with respect and professionalism."*

The group's mission represented its commitment to civility. However, because they knew that reversing a culture of incivility needed the support of leadership, they took their idea to the hospital's administrators. The mission was warmly embraced and the Civility Squad was encouraged to continue their efforts. The administrators even offered a small budget to cover the cost of researching the problem and developing evidence-based practice solutions.

An outside research company was hired to survey the entire staff about job satisfaction, ideas about professionalism and the perception of civility in the workplace. The researchers also analyzed employee turnover statistics. The results of the survey helped shape the interventions developed by Heather's group.

With the help of the organization's attorneys, the team drafted a strict "zero-tolerance" policy on uncivil and disruptive behaviors. It defined the problem, outlined the protocol for reporting the behaviors and clearly stated the consequences. The hospital adopted the policy and every existing employee (along with all future new employees) had to read and sign it.

Next, the Civility Squad organized a "Buddy Listener Line" for employees having problems with bullying in the workplace. The confidential line was staffed by trained mediators and experts in conflict resolution who would listen to the employee's problem and identify the most appropriate action for the circumstances.

And, finally, the team developed a mandatory training program for all staff on appropriate professional behavior. It covered all the topics found throughout the chapters of this book.

Change came slowly…but it came! Over the course of the next two years, a majority of the staff received the training and the "zero-tolerance" policy was being enforced. The outside research company was brought back to survey the staff on employee satisfaction again and to take another look at employee turnover rates.

The results of the survey were positive and the Civility Squad was given the go-ahead to continue the programs. Heather felt satisfied! She knew she was making a difference for the healthcare workers who would come after her. This was her "pay it forward" work.

Now It's Your Turn

Heather's example is just *one* way to create a more civil workplace. No single solution will be right for every organization. It's your job to find out what is needed in your workplace.

Take a moment right now and write down all the things that frustrate you or make your job difficult (or even impossible). List anything you have observed that may be harmful to yourself, your co-workers and your patients. Be sure to consider all those interpersonal issues (like conflict and bullying) that distract you or get in the way of your ability to do your job. List every single issue that comes to mind.

THE PROBLEMS I'VE IDENTIFIED INCLUDE:

1. _____

_____

2. _____

_____

3. _____

_____

4. _____

_____

5. _____

_____

6. _____

_____

7. _____

_____

8. _____

_____

9. _____

_____

10. _____

_____

Now, narrow it down. Place a star next to your top three issues. They will serve as the starting point for you to initiate change—and pay it forward.

Define the Consequences

Take your top three issues and dig deeper into why these issues matter. For a problem to be worthy of your time and energy, it must have some clearly identifiable consequences. Ask yourself, does this issue lead to harm of patients or workers in any way? Does it lead to increased employee turnover? Does it cause waste in time or money? Here's an example:

The Problem: The healthcare teams from the day shift and the night shift do not get along. They engage in constant bickering and backstabbing as each team insists it is the harder working of the two.

The Consequences: Because of the distrust between the two teams, staff members are wasting precious time double checking the previous shift's work. It has become a nasty game—to see who can spot the most mistakes. As a result, team members are spending less time caring for patients. A significant number of patients have expressed dissatisfaction with their care. Medical errors have increased on both shifts. One staff member has been fired and three more are threatening to quit.

NOW YOU TRY IT!

(Feel free to use a separate sheet of paper if you need more room!)

Problem #1: _____

_____

The Consequences: _____

_____

_____

Problem #2: _____

_____

The Consequences: _____

_____

_____

Problem #3: _____

_____

The Consequences: _____

_____

_____

Brainstorm the Solutions

"Nobody can go back and start a new beginning,
but anyone can start today and make a new ending."
~ Maria Robinson

It's time to "triage" your identified problems. Decide the order in which you should tackle the issues. Should you start with the problem causing the most serious consequences? Or does one problem clearly feed into the others? Once you've picked your top challenge, your job is to come up with a few creative (but possible) solutions!

You may already have a clear solution in your mind. If so, that's great! But, you also need to do a little research and come up with more than one idea. Talk to your co-workers and supervisor, look online for examples of how others have solved the same or similar issues. Talk to colleagues who work in different areas or for a different employer. Find out how they would solve the problem.

Define your possible solutions here!

ISSUE #1: _____

POSSIBLE SOLUTIONS: _____

_____

_____

_____

ISSUE #2: _____

POSSIBLE SOLUTIONS: _____

_____

_____

_____

ISSUE #2: _____

POSSIBLE SOLUTIONS: _____

_____

_____

_____

Muster Support and Identify Key Players

As you collected information about the possible solutions to your problem(s), did you identify a few sources of *support* for your cause? Remember, there is power in numbers. The more supporters you have, the more likely you will succeed in your mission.

So, gather a group of individuals who share your problem, see the consequences and *believe* in your solutions. Let them know what you are doing and request their support when and if you need it.

Where Do You Go from Here?

Now, it's time to take your ideas to the decision makers. But who are the decision makers? That's what you have to figure out next!

It may be as simple as going to your supervisor. Or, that may be the first of many steps. Depending on your exact issue, you may need to go to Human Resources, to the Ethics Committee or to the Infection Control office. You may need to speak to the head of your department, to an administrative assistant or to the president of your organization.

If your issue has more wide-reaching public consequences, involving more than your workplace, you may find yourself contacting the governor of your state or your representatives in the Senate.

The key is to get your issue and your ideas heard by the person (or people) who can actually help fix the problem! Ponder your choices and discuss it with your supporters. Then fill in the blanks below.

WHO ARE YOUR KEY PLAYERS (OR DECISION-MAKERS)?

1. _____

2. _____

3. _____

"Individual commitment to a group effort—that is what makes a team work, a company work, a society work, a civilization work."
~Vince Lombardi

Get Prepared

Once you identify your key decision-makers, your next step is to prepare what you need to say to them. Once you've got your "talking points" down, make an appointment and go for it!

Here are some tips to help you get ready:

Clearly identify the problem. Don't beat around the bush. Chances are the decision-makers will be busy people who are short on time. So, state your problem briefly and concisely. Prepare one or two simple sentences that get right to the root of the matter.

Highlight the consequences. Once you pinpoint your problem, say, "This issue deserves attention because..." Then, highlight every consequence you identified.

Offer your solutions. Again, being brief but concise, describe your ideas for potential solutions. If possible, use specific incidents and/or evidence to back up your ideas. For example, your evidence might come from employee turnover statistics, patient satisfaction surveys, studies conducted by the Performance Improvement department at your workplace or information from a professional organization or a reputable source on the internet. (See page 145 for more resource ideas.)

Hand over the ball. Now the ball is in the decision-makers court! Be prepared to answer tough questions and possibly even have your ideas rejected. You may be asked to gather more support or more evidence. Or, you may be told that there is no money available to implement your idea. However, you must also be prepared for the decision-makers say, "Okay, let's do it!" Then, it's time to get to work making your changes.

"If nothing ever changed, there'd be no butterflies."
~Author Unknown

✳ **Review What You've Learned!** ✳

- The healthcare system is fraught with underlying problems that have led to a widespread culture of incivility.

- YOU know exactly what's wrong with the system because you're on the front lines fighting the battle every day.

- Healthcare workers are the largest group of employees in a single industry. Because there is power in numbers, you have the ability to change the system.

- Shared Governance is a way to empower every member of the healthcare team to influence decision-making. And professional organizations have the resources and strategies to bring your voice to the policy makers.

- You must be willing to step out of your comfort zone and work with your peers. Together, you can find solutions to the problems that are fueling incivility in the healthcare environment.

"Don't wait for people to be friendly;
show them how."
~Author Unknown

✳ **Food for Thought** ✳

- When you are in a rut at work, what helps you get out of it? (Maybe you can use that knowledge to motivate your co-workers to work toward change.)

- How do you see your healthcare career progressing? What would you like to be doing, career-wise, in five years? Ten years? What can you do now to make sure you reach your goals?

- Do you think of yourself as more of a *leader* or a *follower*? How can you make use of this knowledge as you begin your "pay it forward" work?

Now, Go Get 'Em!

In the legendary words of the Once-ler from Dr. Seuss's The Lorax,

> *"Unless someone like you cares a whole awful lot,*
> *nothing's going to get better. It's not."*

Take your knowledge, your enthusiasm, your ideas and your civility out of hiding! This industry NEEDS to hear from you. We've said it before, but it's worth repeating: We are glad you chose a career in healthcare—and we want you to stay.

So, "just say no" to the culture of incivility that persists throughout healthcare workplaces everywhere. Even if you find yourself smack in the middle of rude, thoughtless or disrespectful co-workers, you have the power (and bear the responsibility) to control your reaction to them. Look beyond their behavior to identify the underlying causes of incivility in your workplace. Then, band together to make the changes needed for a kinder, gentler workplace.

Today is your day to embrace civility and make working in healthcare better—for you, for your co-workers and for the next generation of healthcare employees. It all starts with you!

Notes

Notes

Notes

Notes

References and Resources

To learn more about how to improve the healthcare environment by embracing a culture of civility, check out the resources we used in developing this book.

Chapter 1: Why Civility Matters

- "Workplace bullying in nursing: a problem that can't be ignored," J. S. Murray

- "The bullying aspect of workplace violence in nursing," M. Johnston, P. Phanhtharath and B. S. Jackson

- "Bullying, incivility, and disruptive behaviors in the healthcare setting: identification, impact, and intervention," D. M. Felblinger

- "Identifying and addressing bullying in nursing," M. Cleary, G. E. Hunt and J. Horsfall

- Institute for Safe Medication Practices. Survey on workplace intimidation. 2003. Available at: http://www.ismp.org/pressroom/pr20040331.pdf

- "Disruptive clinical behavior: a persistent threat to patient safety," G. Porto and R. Lauve

- "The Cost of Bad Behavior: How Incivility Is Damaging Your Business and What to Do About It," Christine Pearson and Christine Porath

- "On the nature, consequences and remedies of workplace incivility: No time for "nice"? Think again," Christine Pearson and Christine Porath. Published by Academy of Management Executive, 2005, Vol. 19, No. 1

Chapter 2: It Starts with You!

- Dr. P. M. Forni's Civility Website at krieger.jhu.edu/civility

- The Institute for Civility in Government at www.instituteforcivility.org

- The Civility Institute at www.civilityinstitute.com

- The Joint Commission at www.jointcommission.org

Chapter 3: Do What You Say and Say What You Mean

- The International Centre for Nursing Ethics at www.nursing-ethics.org

- Josephson Institute of Ethics at www.josephsoninstitute.org

- American Journal of Bioethics at www.ajobonline.com

- The Center for Bioethics and Human Dignity at http://www.cbhd.org

- Learn Well at www.learnwell.org/reality.htm

- *Nursing Ethics Through the Life Span* by Elsie L. Bandman and Bertram Bandman

Chapter 4: Good Fences Make Great Neighbors

- Abraham Maslow, Father of Modern Management, www.abraham-maslow.com

- Healthcare Trainer, June Fabre, www.junefabre.com

- "Why Co-workers Don't Make Good Facebook Friends," found at: www.careerealism.com/co-workers-facebook-friends

Chapter 5: Working in the Salad Bowl

- *Managing to Have Fun,* Matt Weinstein

- *Stressed Out about Communication Skills*, Kathleen Bartholomew RN, MN

- *New Nurse's Survival Guide,* Genevieve Chandler

- "Team Building in Primary Healthcare - A Resource Guide," found at: www.qiip.ca/tbrg.php

- "Using Humor in the Workplace: Understanding the Importance of Healthy Workplace Humor as a Tool to Develop Positive Relationships," www.pennbehavioralhealth.org/documents/ humor_in_the_workplace.pdf

Chapter 6: Eliminate Gossip and Bullying

- The Workplace Bullying Institute, found at: www.workplacebullying.org

- The Joint Commission, found at: www.jointcommission.org

- "A Matter of Respect and Dignity: Bullying in the Nursing Profession," Laura A. Stokowski, RN, MS

- "The Downward Spiral: Incivility in Nursing," Laura Stokowski, RN, MS

Chapter 7: You Can't Always Get What You Want

- *Coping with Difficult People*, Robert M. Bramson, Ph.D.

- *Since Strangling Isn't an Option*, Sandra A. Crowe, M.A.

- *Assertiveness Step By Step,* Windy Dryden

- *The Assertiveness Handbook,* Mary Hartley

- *Zapping Conflict in the Health Care Workplace,* Dr. Judith Briles

- University of Wisconsin, Dept. of Human Resources at www.ohrd.wisc.edu

- Christine Kemp-Longmore, The Black Collegian Magazine at www.black-collegian.com

- Daniel Robin & Associates, www.abetterworkplace.com

- Arlyne Diamond, www.conflictresolutionblog.com

- Mindtools at www.mindtools.com

- www.sideroad.com.

Chapter 8: Taking It to the Extreme

- "Newly Licensed RNs' Characteristics, Work Attitudes, and Intentions to Work," by C. T. Kovner, C. S. Brewer, S. Fairchild, S. Poornima, H. Kim and M. Djukic

- Civility Matters: Leading the Coalition of Change: Creating and Sustaining Communities of Civility. Found at: hs.boisestate.edu/civilitymattersAnger Management Online at: http://angermanagementonline.com

- The American Psychological Association at: www.apa.org/topics/anger/control.aspx

- Get the Angries Out at: www.angriesout.com

- Meditation Works at: www.meditation-works.com

- Guide to Self at: www.guidetoself.com

- The Mayo Clinic at: www.mayoclinic.com

- The Institute for the Prevention of Workplace Violence at: www.workplaceviolence911.com

- OSHA's information on workplace violence at: http://www.osha.gov/SLTC/workplaceviolence/index.html

Chapter 9: Paving the Path to Civility

- *The Civility Solution: What to Do When People Are Rude,* Dr. P. M. Forni

- *The 10 Foundations of Motivation: How to Get Motivated and Stay Motivated,* Shawn Doyle

- American Nurses Association: www.nursingworld.org

- Reflections on Nursing Leadership:
  www.reflectionsonnursingleadership.org

- The Nursing Times: www.nursingtimes.net

- Happy at Work Project at www.workhappynow.com

Resources for Getting Involved

Here are a few key websites and organizations that may be helpful to you as you work toward changing and improving your workplace and your profession:

- Agency for Healthcare Research and Quality: www.ahrq.gov

- American Nurses Association: www.nursingworld.org

- Center for Evidence Based Medicine: www.cebm.net

- Centers for Medicare and Medicaid Services: www.cms.gov

- Commonwealth Fund: http://www.commonwealthfund.org

- Department of Health and Human Services: www.hhs.gov

- Institute of Medicine: www.iom.edu

- National Council of State Legislatures: www.ncsl.org

- RN Activist Kit: www.rnaction.org

- United States Department of Labor: www.dol.gov

- United States House of Representatives: www.house.gov

- United States Senate: www.senate.gov

Index

Meet the Authors

Linda H. Leekley, BS, RN began her nursing career in the oncology department at Duke University Medical Center. After experience in acute care, home health, clinical education and healthcare writing, she founded the healthcare publishing company, In The Know, in 1998. Linda believes that civility and lifelong learning are the keys to both personal and professional success. She welcomes feedback from her readers at lindaleekley@knowingmore.com.

Stacey L. Turnure, RN came into nursing as a second career. It was in response to her mother's diagnosis and eventual death from cancer that inspired the career change. Now, a nurse educator, healthcare education writer and double-time mom to twin boys, Stacey looks forward to inspiring others to follow their dreams, use their voices and make positive changes where change is so desperately needed. Readers may reach Stacey at staceyturnure@knowingmore.com.